THE FATHER'S BLESSING

John Arnott

BOOKS ABOUT S
ORLANDO

D1017883

Creation House
Strang Communications Company
600 Rinehart Road
Lake Mary, FL 32746
Fax: (407) 333-7100

Unless otherwise noted, all Scripture quotations are from the
New International Version of the Bible. Copyright © 1973,
1978, 1984, International Bible Society. Used by permission.

Scripture quotations marked KJV are from
the King James Version of the Bible.

Scripture quotations marked TLB are from The Living
Bible. Copyright © 1971. Used by permission of Tyndale
House Publishers Inc., Wheaton, IL 60189. All rights reserved.

Scripture quotations marked NKJV are from the New King
James Version of the Bible. Copyright © 1979, 1980, 1982
by Thomas Nelson Inc., publishers. Used by permission.

To my precious wife, Carol.
God used you to heal and restore me,
and you taught me to love and forgive.

To the people at Jubilee Vineyard Christian
Fellowship of Stratford, Ontario, on whom I
practiced for twelve years, endeavoring to
learn how to pastor and discover the
principles of the kingdom of God.

To the people of the Vineyard Christian
Fellowship — Toronto Airport. You've
welcomed this fresh move of the Holy Spirit
and have excitedly and lovingly taken the
main load of ministering to the nations and
endeavored to "give it away." Without you
"the Toronto blessing" would not have been possible.

To Christians, pastors and leaders who have
traveled to Toronto in search of more of
the grace of life and have found refreshing,
healing and renewal at the touch of the Master's hand.

ACKNOWLEDGMENTS

To Billy Graham and his organization who
brought me to Christ forty years ago with the
help of my mother and grandfather.

To the Pentecostal churches in Toronto who
taught a Baptist boy that there was more.

To Kathryn Kuhlman who showed me
God's loving power in action.

To Benny Hinn who loves Jesus and the
Holy Spirit more than anyone else I know.

To Mark Virkler who helped me hear the voice of the Lord.

To John and Paula Sandford who evangelized my heart.

To John Wimber who taught me anyone, even me,
could move in the power of the Holy Spirit.

To Claudio Freidzon who prayed
for me and imparted faith and power.

To Randy Clark who brought great blessing to Toronto.

To Christians around the world who have
relentlessly prayed for revival in our day.

To Christina Williams who took my
transcripts and made them all make sense.

To our Lord Jesus Christ who is my Savior and
friend who sticks closer to me than a brother.

To the Holy Spirit who, even when
I am unfaithful, is faithful still.

To God the Father who, according to His sovereign
wisdom and love, planned it all and has given us
"the Father's blessing."

CONTENTS

INTRODUCTION

Since you are reading this book, you have probably heard of "the Toronto blessing." This term was coined by some creative British journalists to describe the renewal services that have been happening at our church, the Toronto Airport Vineyard, since January 1994.

But really, it's "the Father's blessing" because this wonderful outpouring comes from Him. Thankfully, it's not confined to Toronto.

As pastor of this church, and with the nightly meetings we've had for a year and a half, it has been difficult to find time to put my thoughts about everything that's been occurring on paper. But I am delighted to have this opportunity to share with you what God is doing in our midst.

We know that controversy has accompanied this move of God. I can understand people feeling cautious because I felt much of that same apprehension at first. But as I saw the fruit, as I understood previous revivals in church history and as I reread certain biblical texts, I became convinced that we were and are in the midst of a powerful move of God.

Now this anointing is being carried to England, Switzerland, Germany and the rest of Europe; it has gone to Australia, New Zealand, India, Southeast Asia, Korea, Japan, Zimbabwe and South Africa just to name a few places. Thousands of pastors come to be refreshed by God, then they take this back to their churches and pour out the refreshing on their people. It is a fire that is "gloriously" beyond our ability to contain.

I have written this book to share the wonder and awe of the Father's blessing and manifest presence with you. I want you to know what He's been showing us. The first section is about the foundation we need to build this renewal on — God's love and joy, the person of the Holy Spirit and the value of humility. The second section is about what has been happening in our church — the phenomena you've been hearing about and the fruit of these phenomena. The last section tells how to make the Holy Spirit feel welcome, what you can do to enter in and how this renewal is spreading around the world.

Throughout the book I have included first-hand testimonies of people who have visited us. I know you will be astonished at how God has loved and healed His church. I hope you will choose to enter into this renewal with us.

Admittedly, this book is speaking more to the heart than the head. So much more would need to be written if I were attempting to say all that should be said about every topic. Writing on the Holy Spirit alone would require several volumes before it could be called thorough in any way.

This book is not an attempt to address manifold and complex theological issues, nor do I wish to imply that we have all the answers or that this renewal is without problems. Much of what the Holy Spirit does and why He does it is still very much a mystery. For the present we see "through a glass, darkly" (1 Cor. 13:12, KJV).

This book is an attempt, rather, to awaken your heart to realize that our God is an awesome God and that the church desperately needs a revival. God is never limited by circumstances; however, He is moving in great power around the world in every nation and denomination. He is pouring out His Spirit on all flesh, and His sons and daughters are prophesying and dreaming dreams (Joel 2:28), and they are being transformed in their hearts.

This renewal is primarily a call to the "weak ones" rather than to the "wise." It is a call to the thirsty to come and drink of the waters of life freely, to partake of that which is revealed to babes (Matt. 11:25). Our Father is calling His children who deeply desire more of God and who will come in childlike faith to enter into the kingdom (Matt. 18:4-6) and receive the Father's promised blessing (Acts 1:4).

This is a season for "wise virgins" to buy oil from those who sell (Matt. 25). May you be filled with all the fullness of God and powerfully prepared for the harvest. ✪

PART I

FOUNDATIONAL ISSUES
OF THE HEART

CHAPTER 1

GOD'S LOVE:
THE BOTTOM LINE

I had met him two days before. His name was David, which was appropriate since he was a pastor in Israel. David was skeptical about what was happening in our church, but he spent fourteen hours on the plane to come to Toronto anyway.

David was touched in a way he never dreamed possible. When I interviewed him in front of the church that night, he told us, "I've been pastoring for about six years. It's been so hard, especially where I live in Israel. There's tremendous resistance and spiritual warfare. I was just drained and exhausted. I came here really desperate. I couldn't carry on anymore."

David was shaking and his knees were buckling intermittently as he described what happened to him in our church. "I felt like the Father was holding me in His arms, playing with me, tossing me on His knees...just waves of love." He started crying softly as he told us, "He's telling me that He loves and He cares for me."

LOVE IS NUMBER ONE

David met the God of love in person that night. That was just what David needed. Love is what we all need, isn't it? Even God wants to be loved (Deut. 6:5), and He wants to put His love in our hearts.

Jesus confirmed that love is the bottom line when He was asked what the greatest commandment was.

> Jesus replied, "'Love the Lord your God with all your heart and with all your soul and with all your mind.' This is the first and greatest commandment. And the second is like it: 'Love your neighbor as yourself.' All the Law and the Prophets hang on these two commandments" (Matt. 22:37-40).

Jesus did not pick one of the Ten Commandments as being the most important. Instead, Jesus revealed that the greatest, most valuable thing we have been given to do is to love the Lord and love one another. We are in the business of building the kingdom of love. Will we love Him with all of our heart, soul, strength and mind, and will we love one another?

What does it look like when we love the Lord with all our heart and soul?

SERVICE IS NOT A SUBSTITUTE FOR A LOVE AFFAIR

The question now is, How do we love God when we cannot see Him? How do we love Him when it is difficult to get in touch with Him intellectually and mentally, let alone emotionally? I think this challenge often leads us to substitute serving God for loving God.

We think, "If I work hard for God, that means I love Him." Our culture promotes this. We are a very goal-setting, results-oriented people. But that is not all the Lord had in mind. When Jesus summarized the law in two sentences, He was saying, "God wants to have a profound, emotional and meaningful relationship with you, and He wants you to have the same with others." He is calling for heart-to-heart relationships, not merely head-to-head.

If we will enter into these kinds of relationships, everything else in the kingdom of God will fall into place because the whole law and the prophets depend on how loving and lovable we are. Relationship takes precedence over service. Our good works do not prove we have an intimate, heartfelt love affair with Him.

I recently spoke at the Intercessors for Canada conference in Hamilton, Ontario. During the testimony time, Pearl MacNearney from Nova Scotia told of a vision she had during the ministry time.

> Jesus and I were in my mother's hayfield. We were holding hands, and I was skipping along beside and in front of Him. I was about eight to ten years old with my hair in pigtails. He was absolutely delighted with me, as I was with Him. I could hardly believe He was enjoying Himself. Every so often I would turn around and look at Him as if to say, "Is this OK? Am I allowed to do this?" His eyes, filled with love, said, "I am as thrilled with

you as you are with Me." Something pierced my heart during this vision. He revealed Himself to me as friend and brother.

After Pearl shared this vision at the conference, I prayed that she would never work for the Lord again, but work with Him. Pearl wrote me, "The Lord is doing a work in His body, restoring His people to love Him and Him alone. He is replacing the work ethic with the love ethic!"

How do we know Jesus wants this love relationship? Listen to His message to His church in Ephesus:

> I know your deeds, your hard work and your perseverance. I know that you cannot tolerate wicked men, that you have tested those who claim to be apostles but are not, and have found them false. You have persevered and have endured hardships for my name, and have not grown weary (Rev. 2:2-3).

This sounds like a very hard-working church, doesn't it? Jesus praises them for their good deeds, their hard work and perseverance. They were discerning about false prophets and wickedness in their church. They endured hardship without falling away or getting tired of it. What a great church! They had it all together. Many of us would love to be in a church like that, right?

> Yet I hold this against you: You have forsaken your first love (v. 4).

Jesus tells them that, regardless of their great actions, they have forsaken — left, walked away from — their first love, their love for Him.

> Remember the height from which you have fallen! (v. 5).

15

Jesus reminds them that they used to be up in the heights of romance. Now they have fallen down. They used to be radically in love with Him, but now they are just working for Him. His solution?

> Repent and do the things you did at first. If you do not repent, I will come to you and remove your lampstand from its place (v. 5).

This does not sound too good to me. What little light they had was going to be removed if they did not return to Jesus as their first love.

It is not work and achievement that please Him; being in love with Him pleases Him. Then we will work for Him as we used to when we first fell in love with Him. I believe that people who are in love with Jesus will outperform others, don't you? Love is crucial.

He is examining the motive of the heart, not merely the works of the hands.

Let me put this in practical terms. How would you feel if you asked someone to marry you and this was the reply: "Yes, I'll marry you. But I do not want any of that emotional stuff. I do not like it when you put your arms around me or kiss me or that kind of thing. I just want to be practical. I will work for you, make money, take care of the house and the kids and everything else, but do not try to kiss me or be intimate with me."

Would you be anxious to marry that person? Is that what you want in a spouse? No. It isn't what Jesus wants in His bride either. He wants a bride who loves Him and then serves Him *because* she loves Him.

DOCTRINE IS NOT A SUBSTITUTE FOR A LOVE AFFAIR

It came as a tremendous revelation to me several years ago that the Christian faith is all about love and "romance"

16

or intimacy. I used to think it was all about understanding the truth and getting our doctrine straight. I believed if we could only have the purity of doctrine the early church had, that would bring God's presence and power. But the early church didn't have their doctrine totally together either.

Paul rebuked Peter publicly for vacillating on whether he was under Jewish law or free from it (Gal. 2:11-14). Disputes arose about customs regarding circumcision and eating, and the early church members had questions on several issues, including whether the Gentiles could be saved. They did not have their doctrine all figured out. Why do you think we have thousands of different denominations today? It is because people believe *their* doctrine is more right than the next person's. But that does not emphasize love. So what is pure doctrine, anyway?

God is love. That is pure doctrine. That is truth.

Don't misunderstand me. The truth that is in Christ Jesus is very important. It is the truth that sets us free (John 8:32). But if ever we have truth without love, we no longer have the truth (1 John 4:8,16).

We look for words that best describe God — holy, omnipotent, omniscient, omnipresent. These all sound very theological, but do they touch your heart deeply?

God is love. He is your Wonderful Counselor, your Everlasting Father who never leaves you or forsakes you (Is. 9:6). He is the Father Himself who tenderly loves you (John 16:27). His unfailing love for you will never be shaken (Is. 54:10). Jesus is the Binder of broken hearts, the Comforter of all who mourn, the One who gives beauty in exchange for ashes, gladness for mourning and praise for despair (Is. 61:1-3). He is love itself, and He wants to love you on a personal and emotional basis.

This is a call to "romance," a call to having a deeper intimate relationship with Jesus. Being in love with Jesus is more important than having pure, perfect doctrine. As we grow with Christ, our doctrine changes, in hopes that it will mature and get closer to the truth. But continually striving after perfect doctrine without generous portions of grace and love will only turn us into pharisaical legalists who fight continually with one another.

I notice that as the Spirit of God sweeps over people, it doesn't seem to matter which church they belong to. Catholics, Anglicans, Pentecostals, Baptists, United Church, Methodists — you name it — come to our church. It makes no difference to the Holy Spirit. He comes and touches them all. He is the only true source of unity. He enables us to hold our distinctives without breaking fellowship. His unity is based on relationship, not on sameness and conformity.

Many people who come to our services receive a revelation of God's love for them. That was what Eleanor Buckingham wanted when she and her husband, both former pastors, traveled from Washington to visit our church in September 1994. She told us in a letter, "My cry for a long time had been to love God with all my heart, but I just felt a blockage."

My wife, Carol, prayed for her husband, then for Eleanor, who relates, "While I was on the floor (jerking), I saw and felt the river of life and love flowing from the throne into my life and returning again to Jesus, but branching out on both sides in compassion and love. The cry of my heart was answered and I realized for the first time what it meant to love Jesus because He first loved me."

Eleanor saw it, she felt it, she experienced it. This is a foundational issue: being profoundly in love with Jesus.

SITTING AT HIS FEET

What would you do if Jesus and at least twelve other men showed up at your house and they looked hungry? Two sisters, Martha and Mary, faced this situation. What did each choose?

"Martha was distracted by all the preparations that had to

be made" (Luke 10:40). She ran around checking the roast, setting the table, trying to get the meal ready.

What was Mary doing? "Mary...sat at the Lord's feet listening to what he said" (v. 39). Mary was resting at the feet of Jesus, saying, "Ahhhh, what wisdom. Jesus, You're wonderful!"

Martha became angrier and angrier until finally she demanded that Jesus tell her sister to help her get the meal ready. She needed to make Him see that this was not fair at all. But Jesus responded:

> Martha, Martha, you are worried and upset about many things, but only one thing is needed. Mary has chosen what is better, and it will not be taken away from her (vv. 41-42).

What Mary was doing was more important than scurrying around getting food prepared. It was more important than being a good hostess, more important even than eating.

Take time every day to sit at the feet of Jesus. He is the Lord of the harvest, but He is also the Lord of the Sabbath.

We are so busy trying to stay on top of the details of life that somehow we get things all mixed up. We think that loving God equals studying the Bible for hours or sacrificing time and money for ministry or some other form of good works. But as Paul said in 1 Corinthians 13, without love, all these works and sacrifices amount to nothing. It's not so much doing good things that please Him, but rather our motives and reasons for doing them. (To understand this further, please read and study 1 Corinthians 13 in two or three different versions as a devotional.)

Let's look at Revelation 2:5 again, this time from The Living Bible.

> Think about those times of your first love (how different now!) and turn back to me again and work as you did before.

Do you remember what you were like when you were first saved? Do you remember how things looked and felt the next day? The grass was greener, the sky was bluer; every person on the face of the earth was a wonderful human being. You were seeing through eyes that had freshly fallen in love. This is what Jesus wants for you.

JESUS WANTS A LOVE AFFAIR WITH YOU

When renewal started happening in our church during the ministry time on January 20, 1994, almost 80 percent of the people were on the floor, laughing, rolling and having the greatest time. I thought, "Lord, this is great. I am glad we are getting a little happier and more joyful. We needed to lighten up, but let us get on with the job of getting people converted!"

Others would even say to me, "This is supposed to be a move of God? How many people are getting saved?"

"People are being saved. We had five saved last night," I responded.

"That's not a revival. A revival is when hundreds of people get saved and the community is impacted!"

At first I agreed. I told the Lord I wanted to see people come to Jesus, to see them healed. So I started preaching more on salvation, but after the sermons, I noticed that the ministry time was difficult.

I didn't understand that. The Holy Spirit was not flowing, and the people were not receiving from the Lord the same as before. The number of people who came to Christ was not as great as it was when I had talked about the joy of the Lord or the love of God or phenomena in the Bible. I asked the Lord why. I was surprised by His response:

"It is because you are pushing Me."

"Lord, I don't want to push You. What do You mean?"

His reply floored me: "Is it all right with you if I just love on My church for a while?"

That kind of response causes us to wonder: "Why would He want to love us? We know what we are really like."

It seems that God has a great desire: to love and to be loved.

This kind of romance cannot be explained. Why does my wife, Carol, love me? I ask her all the time, "Honey, what do you see in me? Why do you love me?" She gives me all of her reasons, but they don't totally satisfy me. I am still puzzled. Most of us do not think we are lovable, but Jesus is radically in love with you, and He wants to come and fill your life, bless you, transform you and fully win your heart.

We as a people have proven we're not good at loving Him, and we are worse at loving one another. But since Jesus desperately wants a bride who loves Him with abandonment, He's graciously filling our hearts beyond capacity. As a result, our love for Him is constantly increasing. Love must be experienced before it goes deeper; it cannot stay in the theoretical realm. The Holy Spirit is bringing this experience to us now. When He fills you with His love, you will become a lover, too — His love will pour out of you to others.

Dr. Margaret Poloma, a professor in the sociology department at the University of Akron in Ohio, is presently doing a study on our church. She pointed out to me that religion is not an objective institution only with particular doctrines and rituals, but also must involve subjective, emotional experiences. In summarizing Abraham Maslow, a late renowned psychologist who wrote a book in the sixties titled *Religion, Values, and Peak Experience,* Margaret says that "institutional religion is about non-peakers teaching non-peakers about the peak experiences of others." In other words, people who place no subjective, religious experiences for themselves are teaching others who likewise are skeptical about emotional responses to what they profess to be learning. What are they studying? Christians are often pondering and discussing the peak experiences of great Old Testament figures like Abraham and Moses or New Testament disciples like Peter and Paul.

There is a major flaw in their logic. The Christian church desperately needs a reality check. We are suggesting that we need to be both objective and subjective if we are going to have an intimate and personal relationship with Christ. Someone once summarized it this way: "It is better felt than 'telt'."

Nicki Gerster of Frankfurt, Germany, came to our meetings and had her own experience with God. This is how she described what happened to her one night during worship:

> I fell in love with Jesus afresh. It was like a moment of looking straight into His loving eyes. I'm still stunned by this experience.

God is not trying to trick you into a life of servitude, saying, "Aha! I've got you now. You made a commitment at the front of that church. It is all written down in heaven, and I am going to hold you to your word." He is not trying to con you into going to farthest Africa or some place to die in the jungle for the gospel — but His love might call you there. He wants to draw near and win your heart.

THE FATHER'S LOVE

Most of us are gun-shy about this kind of love and closeness; we don't know what to do with it. It makes people very uncomfortable when we start preaching about intimacy. They say, "Come on. Don't give us that mushy stuff. We want to hear the gospel."

But the funny thing is that this really *is* the gospel. You can read it in John 3:16.

For God so *loved* the world that he gave his one and only Son, that whoever believes in him shall not perish but have eternal life (italics added).

I don't know anybody who would give up their son for someone else. Abraham was willing, but God actually did it. God, the Father, so loved us, so loved *me*, so loved *you*.

Why did I miss it for so many years, not knowing how incredibly loving the Father was? I thought "Jesus is OK, but watch out for God because you can never please Him. He has a list, and wants to talk to you. He's upset because you didn't do it better or you didn't do enough." I thought of the Father in abstract, theological terms. I knew God was love, yet my heart expected Him to be harsh and demanding.

But the Father is just like Jesus. Isn't that what Jesus said?

Anyone who has seen me has seen the Father (John 14:9).

Jesus was in essence saying, "The Father and I are the same; We are one. We have the same heart, the same emotions, the same Spirit; if you have seen Me, and if you love Me, you will love the Father also."

The greatest revelation I hear night after night is that God has come to people by the power of the Holy Spirit and revealed His love to them personally, often through visions and dreams and prophecy. They say, "I know now that my heavenly Father really loves me." Joel 2:28 is being fulfilled before our eyes.

Virginia Smith, a pastor's wife from The City Church in Bellevue, Washington, became newly acquainted with the love the Father had for her on the day of her birthday at our church. One of our staff pastors, Ian Ross, asked Virginia to put her hands over her heart. Then he prayed for healing of her broken heart — a heart broken by the father-images in her life. Ian told Virginia that God would never reject her, that she was accepted by Him. He said that God loved her perfectly, and nothing she could do would make Him love her more. Virginia later wrote to us and said:

> These were not new thoughts to me; I had taught these same truths to women for years. What made this encounter with God so life-changing was the transfer of knowledge from my mind to my spirit. All of a sudden I felt God's love and total acceptance — so much so, I found myself bent forward at the waist, weeping deeply from my innermost being. The tears were not tears of repentance or feelings of self-pity, but cries of joy and gratitude that God could love me so completely.

As Virginia wept, two members of the worship team came and sang over her while a violinist accompanied them. She found herself "paralyzed" by God's anointing in the midst of this circle of worship and love.

> I have never experienced such power and healing. I finally had to ask God to stop because my physical body could no longer tolerate such overwhelming love. I was immediately conscious of my frailty before the Lord and just how little of the Holy Spirit I could contain. Totally exhausted, I dropped to my knees and fell on my face. I felt a great desire to humble myself and rest in His presence. I walked in hungry to know Jesus more intimately and walked out full and overflowing with the goodness and love of God.

Do you know what that experience is worth? It changes everything. We will gladly surrender control to a Father who loves us so profoundly. That revelation breaks the strategy the enemy has so painstakingly built into our lives

— the idea that not even God could love us or that God the Father is not really loving. The lie is exposed and instantly evaporates. Only the Holy Spirit can do that. It is a revelation of the heart.

The Holy Spirit will call you and endeavor to win your heart. He is usually not going to force you; it is an invitation. He knocks on your heart and says, "How would you like to take part in the best thing that has ever been offered to the human race? It is a kingdom of love, a place where everybody loves everybody from the King on down."

But to many people, love is just another four-letter word they don't relate to. I have asked hundreds of people if they ever heard their fathers or mothers say the words "I love you, son" or "I love you, daughter." So many say no.

You might answer, "I know my father never said it. He could not articulate those kind of things, but I know he loved me because we ate every day and we had a home to live in." He worked to support you, but you needed more than that. You may be able to rationalize it intellectually, but in your emotional understanding, no loving, caring, providing, nurturing, affirming father was there for you. This left a deep vacuum. If parents would only emotionally touch and hold and affirm their children, they would grow up much better prepared to respond to the love of God.

Our hearts need to know how wonderful God is and how much He really cares for us. This revelation needs to reach deep into our inner beings.

Kim Beadman found this out when she went to our Catch the Fire — Down Under conference in June 1995 in Sydney, Australia. After being prayed for one night, Jesus came to her in a vision. Kim describes what she and Jesus did in the vision:

> We were running through really beautiful long yellow grass...I noticed I was a little girl again

25

because my hair was very fair, and as I've gotten older, my hair has become dark.

We were laughing and running with our arms spread wide like airplanes. Then we walked through a pond. When we reached the other side, I found myself playing at God's feet with Legos (toy building blocks). God was watching me, and then He was lying beside me playing with them, too. He then took me up and sat me on His knee, and He started to curl His finger around strands of my hair.

You see, when I was a little girl, I always wanted Legos, but my mum could never afford them. I had also longed for someone to play with my hair when I was a child. It was such a precious moment for me; only God really knew how much it meant to me. The most wonderful thing about this vision is that I had forgotten those things that I had really longed for as a little girl. But He showed me that He is my Daddy, and He never forgets. My heavenly Father has shown me that He has always been there; I know He loves me and He knows my deepest needs and desires.

We have tried so hard to be men of God and women of God and never really learned to be children of God. We have emotional needs, and we need to be loved emotionally. Emotions came from our Creator. God has them; He is emotional, and we were made in His image. He wants to love us emotionally; He wants us to love Him emotionally with all our hearts, our souls and as well as our minds (Matt. 22:37).

A LOVING BRIDE

We have a wonderful story in Genesis 24 of Abraham's servant, Eliezer, going to get a bride for Isaac, Abraham's

26

son. This is an allegorical picture of the Holy Spirit going into the world to get a bride for Jesus.

Eliezer traveled to Abraham's old home in Mesopotamia to find Abraham's brother. There he asked God to show him the girl He had chosen for Isaac. Rebekah came to the well with a jar on her shoulder. Eliezer asked her for a drink from the well. Rebekah gave him one and offered to water his camels, too.

Can you imagine how much water ten camels who had just plodded across the desert could drink? I checked with a zoo, and they told me a thirsty camel can gulp down thirty gallons of water at a time. Thirty gallons times ten camels is three hundred gallons of water. Rebekah was really working! Eliezer was surprised and shocked that she did it. But Rebekah had a servant's heart of love, and that was what he was looking for.

Eliezer met her family, then asked if she would go with him and become the wife of his master's son. It was like, "Just leave everything, change your whole lifestyle, forget about what you wanted to do. Leave tomorrow and become a wife to someone you've never met. Yes, that's right. Will you do it?"

It's astounding, but that's the Christian faith. The Holy Spirit comes to you and says, "Will you leave everything you're doing and become a bride to the Master's Son?"

If you agree, there are precious gifts for you, but there's also that camel ride back to Israel. That is where most of us are right now.

Have you ever ridden on a camel? When the camel gets up, it almost throws you over its head. You just catch your balance when it gets up on its front legs, and you almost go over backward. When it's all the way up, you feel like you're twenty feet in the air, and you're thinking, "Help, Lord!"

The ride is no picnic, but it is symbolic of our lives as the body of Christ on earth — a camel ride across the desert back to where Jesus is. We are on our way to Him. The Holy Spirit called you and brought you gifts, all to be a bride for the Master's Son. It's all about romance, intimacy and relationship.

Jackie Gantea and her family drove from their home in Pennsylvania to our church in Toronto. They attended several meetings, and later she wrote me:

> I really felt as if I spent a honeymoon with Jesus. Even though my precious husband, Lee, was with me and we are united in Jesus Christ, I did not sense Lee's presence. I only sensed Jesus as my groom. He danced with me. He walked with me and talked with me.
>
> I used to picture Jesus way up there. Now, I close my eyes and I can picture Him right next to me. Sometimes He is holding my hand or has His arm around me. He is always loving me.

We are talking here about the King of the universe, the most wonderful person in the world, the kindest, gentlest Lamb of God. Yet, He is the Lion of Judah who is the strongest and the toughest there is, and He is radically in love with you.

BUILDING HIS KINGDOM OF LOVE

One day I was thinking about how much I loved Jesus, and I said, "Jesus, living for You here on earth is great, but I can hardly wait to see You. I want to look into those eyes that are like flames of fire. When we meet, I would like to have twenty-four hours with You so that I can ask all the questions I have ever thought of."

Then I asked Him what He would like to do when we meet, and He answered, "Oh, John, I just want to wash your feet." His answer totally undid me; I was not expecting that. It destroyed me for about two hours. I wept and wept and wept, saying to Him, "What kind of a king are You? You who hold the universe in the palm of Your hand, yet are so loving and caring that You would count the hairs on our heads and wash Your disciples' feet. Lord, I am in. You have hooked me; You have captured me. I want You. I am Yours forever. Never again will I doubt You."

I finally understood that loving us is a priority for Him. People will tell you that the most important thing in the kingdom of God is to get the lost saved. I am not saying that it is not important. It is certainly a flaming passion of my heart, but it is not the *most* important. The most important thing in the kingdom of God is to develop a loving relationship with the Lord, getting to know Emmanuel — God with us. Christ in you is the hope of glory (Col. 1:27). Loving your neighbor comes *after* this.

The Holy Spirit is the One who is building this kingdom of love. This move of the Spirit is first of all about a renewal and refreshing for Christians, finding out what a wonderful loving Savior we have; second, it is about loving our neighbor — evangelism.

When the love of God impacts your heart to the fullest, no mountain is too tall, no ocean too broad, no valley too deep that you would not go through it for Him. That kind of love will cause you to serve like nothing else can. Then, rather than working *for* Him, you are working *with* Him to reach the nations of this world.

I recommend you take all the striving, all the performance and everything you try to do to win His approval, set it aside, and get real with God. Say to Him, "Lord, this is what I am really like on the inside. This is the honest truth. I am going to admit it to You and to myself. I am bankrupt inside. I desperately need to know You love me. I desperately need to be refilled with the Holy Spirit. I am not going to try to fool You or anybody else. I want to get real and be filled with Your Spirit. I'm tired of trying to bring Your kingdom to earth through self-effort (Matt. 6:10). I only want to do what I see You doing (John 5:19). I only want to say what I hear You, Father, saying (John 12:49)."

I pray for you now the prayer the apostle Paul prayed. Maybe you will see it in a new light, knowing that it's possible to know — really know — God's immense love for you.

> I pray that you, being rooted and established in love, may have power, together with all the saints, to grasp how wide and long and high and deep is the love of Christ, and to know this love that surpasses knowledge — that you may be filled to the measure of all the fullness of God (Eph. 3:17-19).✪

CHAPTER 2

THE FELLOWSHIP OF
THE HOLY SPIRIT

Who is this Holy Spirit who fills people's hearts with love for Jesus? What is He like? The Holy Spirit is referred to in Scripture with many metaphors. He is wind; He is water, rain or rivers; He is oil; He is fire.

All of these symbols help us understand this wonderful person whom we cannot see. Jesus said the Holy Spirit is also *another* Counselor who is with us just as Jesus was with the disciples. The Holy Spirit is to be with us forever. Jesus told His disciples just before His crucifixion:

If you love me, you will obey what I command. And I will ask the Father, and he will give you another Counselor to be with you forever — the Spirit of truth. The world cannot accept him, because it neither sees him nor knows him. But you know him, for he lives with you and will be in you (John 14:15-17).

Jesus knew His disciples had the law and the prophets. He knew those of us who would believe later would have the testimony of the disciples and other witnesses to tell us what they heard, saw and experienced about Jesus. But He wanted us to have more than the Word of God — He wanted us to have His Spirit living in us.

Unless I go away, the Counselor will not come to you; but if I go I will send him to you. When he comes, he will convict the world...He will guide you into all truth...He will bring glory to me. (John 16:7-8,13,14).

Those scriptures call the Holy Spirit "He." The Holy Spirit is a person; He is not an "it," and He is not just a power. The Greek word for spirit, *pneuma*, is a neuter word, meaning neither male nor female grammatically.[1] So to be correct here, the text should have used the word *it* when talking about the Spirit. But it seems that the rules of Greek grammar were broken to show that the Holy Spirit is a person.

The Holy Spirit is not a phenomenon or a manifestation or an experience. He is God, the Holy Spirit. God the Spirit desires to come and rest powerfully on you, dwell in you, heal you and transform you, so you can see everything through different eyes and from a different perspective. He is for everyone, and He is for *you* personally.

Sarah Berry of Moretown, Vermont, received a personal

lesson from God on who the Holy Spirit is. She came to our services in February 1995. One night during prayer ministry Sarah was on the floor in the Spirit when Jesus came to her in a vision. He replayed for her a long forgotten lecture from an ancient history class she had taken in college. Her professor was describing a special servant who was only in the homes of wealthy Athenians around the fifth century B.C. This servant's only job was to stay with the son and heir of the family from his boyhood until he became an adult. He was responsible for delivering this son safely into his father's hands at his coming-of-age. Sarah goes on to describe this servant.

> This special servant never left the boy's side. He slept in his room, ate with him, walked him to the gymnasium, to school, to meet his friends — everywhere. His job was so important that he held a special position of respect and honor in the family that no other servant enjoyed. Frequently this servant and the son would form such a close relationship that after the son had gained his inheritance, and the servant's job was finished, he would stay on with the family in an honored position.

As Sarah watched, the professor told the class the Greek word for this servant: *parakletos.* Parakletos means advocate and comforter — which is just what the Holy Spirit is.[2]

The Holy Spirit is not just a power, but a precious, caring, loving, wonderful person who is filled up with a consuming passion: He wants to reveal Jesus to you in a greater and more wonderful way. That is His heart. He wants you to be healed of life's hurts so you can tell others what Jesus did for you. He wants to empower you and fill you with more of His anointing, His power and His presence so you can share the love of Jesus with a broken, hurting world and do it with powerful signs following.

Most people know about the trinity — the Father, Son and Holy Spirit — but they are not clear on who the Holy Spirit is and what He does. He is the presence of God right here, right now, on the earth. The Holy Spirit convicts us of sin, righteousness and judgment. He brings the power that changes lives and introduces people powerfully and personally to Jesus.

The Spirit gives us boldness, anointing and giftedness and increases our love for the Lord Jesus so we will take the good news to the ends of the earth. The focus needs to be, "Oh God, heal me, then empower me so I can give Your grace away."

THE SPIRIT AND THE WORD

Sometimes people who love and study the Word of God fear that those who pursue the Holy Spirit are going to lose the Word in the process. Others fear that if we become too theological, focusing on the Scriptures, we will become legalistic and "mind-oriented," losing or quenching the Spirit in the process.

God is calling us to flow with the Word and flow with the Spirit. They will complement each other. It is not either/or; it is both. The Word and the Spirit must go together. Both the Word and the Spirit will always point to Jesus. The Word lays out God's truth before us, but it is the Holy Spirit that gives us revelation.

We need the Holy Spirit as we read the Bible because:

He has made us competent as ministers of a new covenant — not of the letter but of the Spirit; for the letter kills, but the Spirit gives life (2 Cor. 3:6).

Does that mean if you read and follow the Bible, it will kill you? No. Paul is saying that the law of God reveals that no man is able to keep this law, so everyone is destined for the death penalty. The law is constantly reminding us that we are in a hopeless situation. We will never be good enough to satisfy a perfect God.

> Now if the ministry that brought death, which was engraved in letters on stone, came with glory, so that the Israelites could not look steadily at the face of Moses because of its glory, fading though it was, will not the ministry of the Spirit be even more glorious? (vv. 7-8).

The ministry of the Spirit will produce life in you. You and I die to self and are raised to a new life: "Christ in you, the hope of glory" (Col. 1:27). You can go on in newness of life, and the Word of God becomes something that is alive for you and produces life in you.

Have you ever been reading the Bible, maybe during your quiet time in the morning, and all of a sudden a verse just jumps off the page? Those words become alive to you, so you underline them, thinking, "I did not see that before." That is the interaction of the Holy Spirit and the Word of God, making the Word live for you (2 Cor. 3:6).

That's the promise, and that is the hope we have. When the written words are breathed upon by the Holy Spirit, they produce life and not death.

> The words I have spoken to you are spirit and they are life (John 6:63).

Pastor Emmons from London, Ontario, came to our church conference on the Word of God With Power in March 1995. In his own words, he says:

> I didn't shake, rattle (laugh) or roll, but the living Christ came with such power as I sat under the

Word that He, the Holy Spirit, gently renewed, refreshed and restored my fractured life.

Initially, the Word of God renewed my mind, then gave me such a clear focus and the ability to know the mind of Christ and hear His Word — His voice — again. As the Spirit soaked me in His Word, a tired and broken inner man was refreshed and then restored. Restored, not only in my confidence, but a new, restored faith to trust Him more.

We need the Word and the Spirit. If we have only the Word, the letter of the law without the Spirit, we are usually left with some form of religion devoid of that breath of God that makes it alive. And if we have only the Spirit and lose the Word, we can get out into extremes.

Some people have thought, "Now that the Holy Spirit is here, we don't need the Bible anymore. We'll just be led by Him." But history has proven those people get farther and farther from the truth. They begin justifying sin; then they are in sin, and then they deny things like the divinity of Christ.

Of course, the problem is not with the Holy Spirit, but with us. We see (and hear) "through a glass, darkly" (1 Cor. 13:12, KJV). We need the written Word as our road map, our anchor, our guidepost, our North Star that never moves, that we can steer by. The Bible is sure, steadfast, a rock imbedded that shall not move. The Holy Spirit will never be contrary to God's Word, and we need the Holy Spirit to breathe life into the Word and into the church.

We need to remember also that the Bible is not a person; it is, in fact, written by the person of the Holy Spirit (2 Pet. 1:21).

THE WORD AND THE SPIRIT GLORIFY JESUS

Jesus told the Jews who were persecuting Him:

> You diligently study the Scriptures because you
> think that by them you possess eternal life. These
> are the Scriptures that testify about me, yet you
> refuse to come to me to have life (John 5:39-40).

From that verse we discover the Word of God testifies
about Jesus.

> When the Counselor comes, whom I will send to
> you from the Father, the Spirit of truth who goes
> out from the Father, he will testify about me
> (John 15:26).

This verse tells us the Holy Spirit also testifies about
Jesus. The Holy Spirit wants no credit for Himself. He is not
saying, "Hey what about Me? I'm here too, you know." He
doesn't do that. He always glorifies Jesus.

The purpose of both the Word and the Spirit is to point to
Jesus — always. Can you see how they work together? The
Word points to Jesus; the Spirit points to Jesus. The Spirit
breathes on the Word of God making it alive, always point-
ing to Jesus. The Word is a check and balance tool, correcting and fine-tuning what we believe the Spirit is saying.

New doctrines need to be weighed very carefully. One
thing that thrills me so much with this new outpouring of
the Holy Spirit is that no new doctrines are being taught.
There is nothing new here. The Holy Spirit is simply coming
in ways that glorify Jesus, making truth alive in our hearts.

I've interviewed hundreds of people since this renewal
started. I've asked them, "It's great that you fell and shook
and laughed and rolled and jumped and everything, isn't it?
But what's it done in your heart? What's happening inside?"

And almost everyone has said, "I'm more in love with Jesus than I've ever been before. The Holy Spirit will wake me up in the middle of the night, and I find myself praying for all my friends. And one other thing: I can't put the Bible down — I've just got such a hunger for the Word. I'm understanding it now as I never have before. I just love His Word."

Shawna, an eighteen-year-old from the little town of Arthur, Ontario, started coming to our meetings with her family in October 1994. She wrote me about all that the Holy Spirit did for her: "God poured out His love into my life in a new way. I just soaked in God's presence and laughed; I got drunk" (overcome by the Spirit).

She told me that in the weeks following God began to weed out things in her life that no one else would have thought were wrong. She feels set free and writes, "God has been developing my time with Him, I have an increased hunger for the Word of God, and God gives me such revelation when I read the Bible!"

You see how it works — the Word and the Spirit, they both glorify Jesus. And as I said, if you only pursue the Word of God, you'll dry up. If you only pursue the Spirit, forgetting the Word, you'll blow up. But if you take the Word and the Spirit together, you'll grow up — in Jesus.

MORE OF JESUS

The Holy Spirit is on earth gathering up a bride for the Lord Jesus Christ. When the Holy Spirit comes into your life, do you know what will happen? You will look more like Jesus. You will remind Him of the kind of person Jesus is, full of the fruit of the Spirit — love, joy, peace, gentleness, meekness and self-control.

During prayer time in our meetings we ask people, "What would you like God to do for you?" "Oh, I want the power," some say. Although there is nothing wrong with that, I redirect them just a little. It is the Holy Spirit whom you want, not just power, not just an anointing. He is a precious, sensitive person who loves Jesus with everything that He is. Pray this way: "Oh Holy Spirit, come and make me more like Jesus. Come and make me a child of God who will honor the Word, honor the kingdom and honor heaven. Come and fill me. Lord, it is You who I want, not just Your gifts."

This is the heart of the Holy Spirit, to bring you and me into that kind of relationship. The Holy Spirit is calling you to desire Jesus with every atom of your being, with everything that is within you. You don't have to be afraid to ask your loving heavenly Father to give you more of the Holy Spirit. He will not give you a stone if you ask for bread (Matt. 7:9). He loves you so much that He ransomed your life with the life of Jesus.

LIVING WATER

After a hot desert journey, Jesus and His disciples finally arrived at a well, thirsty and tired. There Jesus talked with a Samaritan woman. The Jews despised the Samaritans. (They had the wrong idea of God. They worshiped at the wrong mountain and the wrong temple.) They had many wrong beliefs, but at the same time they loved God, too.

Jesus asked this woman for a drink of water, then told her one of the most profound truths He ever spoke to anyone.

> If you knew the gift of God and who it is that asks
> you for a drink, you would have asked him and
> he would have given you living water (John 4:10).

It is interesting that He offered her "life" rather than correction, isn't it?

Living water — what does that mean? Jesus is saying that the Holy Spirit is like water which is alive. What does water do? It refreshes. It causes plants and trees to grow. All of nature is dependent on water. Jesus says, "I would have given you the life-giving water of the Spirit."

> If anyone is thirsty, let him come to me and drink. Whoever believes in me, as the Scripture has said, streams of living water will flow from within him (John 7:37-38).

Out of your innermost being, rivers of living water will flow. We tell people all the time, "You cannot give away what you have not first received." You need to soak in this and let the Lord make a deposit deep within your inner being. Let Him "marinate" you in the Holy Spirit. Then allow Him to flow out of you in words and acts of life and blessing, giving His anointing away to everyone you meet. There is plenty for you and plenty to give away.

Lynn Beyler from Madison, Wisconsin, wrote us about a vision she had while attending our first Catch the Fire conference.

> I was before a huge golden door, and glory was streaming out of the top, the bottom and both sides of it. The Lord said, "The glory you are being touched with now is only what is leaking out of the door. I am gently getting your physical being ready to stand when My glory is present. Soon I will open the door."
>
> He encouraged me to come in farther to receive all He has for me. The glory was a stream of love coming out from the door. The Lord showed me a box like a shoe box. I knew my old life was in that box. He said that was where I used to keep Him. He tossed the box into the stream of glory and love, and it flew away.
>
> "Now," He said, "You are free to love people the way I love them. Because you were willing to

take Me out of the box and put your old life in it, I am able to bring you closer to Me. Now we are one together forever. This stream of love is for all mankind to flow in with Me."

Are you hungry? Are you thirsty? "If anyone is thirsty, let him come to me and drink," Jesus said (John 7:37). Jump into the stream!

THE HOLY SPIRIT IS FOR YOU

You can go to God today and ask for more of the Holy Spirit.

Do not be afraid, little flock, for your Father has been pleased to give you the kingdom (Luke 12:32).

What is the kingdom?

For the kingdom of God is not a matter of eating and drinking, but of righteousness, peace and joy in the Holy Spirit (Rom. 14:17).

Ask your Father. Open up your heart. Drink of Him, love and worship Him.

How much more will your Father in heaven give the Holy Spirit to those who ask him! (Luke 11:13).

Get alone with God. Desire more of Him. Have a trusted friend lay hands on you right now and believe for the promise of the Father — which is the Holy Spirit. Come, Lord! Come, Holy Spirit. Give more of Your presence, power and love!

He will come and fill you and immerse you in the Holy Spirit, and out of your innermost being, rivers of living water will flow, transforming your life.

41

ABUNDANT JOY

I have been a pastor since 1981 and have been a Christian since 1955. Yet I have never had so much enjoyment pastoring as I am having now. When this invasion of the Holy Spirit and joy began at our church, we were shocked, to say the least.

We never had to preach over the noise of people laughing, crying and shouting before — yet it was as though the people could not help it. They were so filled with joy.

We were thrilled because God showed up, but we were puzzled about what was happening and why. It took me a while to understand that God absolutely wants His people filled with joy. I didn't know that God believed in parties, but it turns out that He throws the best party in the whole universe!

THE HOLY SPIRIT BRINGS JOY

The Bible says the Holy Spirit is our down payment on heaven (2 Cor. 2:23). And we know that heaven is full of joy. The Holy Spirit and joy go together.

> The kingdom of God is not a matter of eating and drinking, but of righteousness, peace and joy in the Holy Spirit (Rom. 14:17).

When a pastor's wife from California came to our Catch the Fire conference in October 1994, she had been weeping and travailing in the Spirit for months. She said she was a very "serious and heavy" person, so the desire of her heart when she came was to be filled with laughter. She prayed:

> "Lord, I will truly believe this is You if I could only laugh." Most of the leadership, my family and friends have all told me to lighten up and relax...I've tried. Please believe me, I am (or was) normal and would laugh when appropriate, but I could *never, ever, ever make myself laugh.*

On the last night of the conference, a woman from the prayer team asked if she wanted more. She said yes, and the woman prayed for her. She writes,

> The God of glory gave me laughter as I have never laughed before in my entire life. As I realized what *God* was doing, I was weeping for joy. Tears

43

of joy were flying out, and the heartiest, fattest sense of love, joy, exuberance and liberty came over me. I think this went on for at least a half hour. Thank You, God. You save the best for last.

Joy is a fruit of the Holy Spirit (Gal. 5:22). So it should be no surprise to us that people who are filled will the Holy Spirit are full of joy! We may not understand it, or we may not want to be a part of it, but the joy of the Lord is filling those who come to Him as His children.

JOY COMES TO THE CHILDREN OF GOD

The apostles were filled with joy when they returned to tell Jesus what God had done through them after He sent them out to minister in the countryside.

> The seventy-two returned with joy and said, "Lord, even the demons submit to us in your name."
> He replied, "I saw Satan fall like lightning from heaven. I have given you authority to trample on snakes and scorpions and to overcome all the power of the enemy; nothing will harm you. However, do not rejoice that the spirits submit to you, but rejoice that your names are written in heaven" (Luke 10:17-20).

If your name is written in heaven, you are a success already. Jesus told the disciples that was the best reason to rejoice, then He thanked His Father in heaven.

> At that time Jesus, *full of joy through the Holy Spirit*, said, "I praise you, Father, Lord of heaven and earth, because you have hidden these things from the wise and learned and revealed them to little children" (v. 21, italics added).

Jesus is "full of joy through the Holy Spirit" as He shares in His disciples' joy.

When He thanks God, Jesus is not despising knowledge that the wise don't understand, but He is despising the pride of man that comes from having knowledge. He is delighted that God reveals things to His children. Can you be a little child, without having to know all the *whys* and the *wherefores*? Can you look past some of the strange manifestations and realize that God is impacting the hearts and lives of the people with this wonderful joy of the Lord? If you can receive that, He will transform you.

FULLNESS OF JOY

Though I have studied the subject of joy in Scripture many times, I am still amazed at how often the Bible talks about it. The Psalms, Isaiah, the Gospels — the Bible from one end to the other is full of this concept of joy. It must be something God wants us to experience all the time in our walk with Him.

We can almost hear David's excitement in Psalm 4 as he exclaims:

> You have filled my heart with greater joy than
> when their grain and new wine abound (Ps. 4:7).

The psalmist is trying to express the tremendous joy that filled his heart. Imagine the joy of a family when their long awaited harvest of grain and wine are finally in. The joy of the Lord is greater!

God can fill us with joy that's greater than the joy that comes with material abundance, new cars, pay raises or promotions. Or how about a restored marriage — how can the joy of that be measured against material things?

One visitor to our Catch the Fire conference wrote that she and her husband were "hanging onto the last thread" in their marriage. They had been living in separate rooms and were utterly defeated, seeing no hope for their marriage. She notes, however, that she knew "all things are possible in Christ."

While in Toronto, they stayed in the same room together. The second night they were sitting at the little table in their room, talking.

> Then the precious Holy Spirit came upon us, and for forty minutes we laughed. We ended up on the floor laughing so hard. Oh, what healing and restoration has come to our marriage. And that was just a taste of what God had for us. We believe a miracle in our marriage had taken place. Praise God.

Jesus wants our joy to be complete, or full.

> If you obey my commands, you will remain in my love, just as I have obeyed my Father's commands and remain in his love. I have told you this so that my joy may be in you and that your joy many be complete (John 15:10-11).
>
> Until now you have not asked for anything in my name. Ask and you will receive, and your joy will be complete (John 16:24).

Jesus wants to take us from joy to fullness of joy. We've watched it in hundreds of people — a tremendous release of joy and laughter that is initiated by the Spirit and brings great healing and freedom. He wants us to have fullness of joy that comes through answered prayer.

> When the Lord brought back the captives to Zion,
> we were like men who dreamed.

> Our mouths were filled with laughter, our tongues
> with songs of joy.
> Then it was said among the nations, "The Lord has
> done great things for them."
> The Lord has done great things for us, and we are
> filled with joy (Ps. 126:1-3).

Some would say that laughter is not joy, but we can all agree that laughter is a very common expression of joy. He wants us to have joy that fills our mouths with laughter.

> Though you have not seen him, you love him; and
> even though you do not see him now, you believe
> in him and are filled with an inexpressible and
> glorious joy, for you are receiving the goal of your
> faith, the salvation of your souls (1 Pet. 1:8-9).

This joy is so rich, so good, so powerful that you cannot even begin to describe it.

The pastors from a church in Pennsylvania wrote me that an "unusually quiet" woman in their congregation went home after a service and laughed in the Spirit for an hour. The woman then realized that it had been five years to the day that her sister died from cancer. The Lord told her that she would never grieve her sister's death again. Joy is a healing balm, too.

> The ransomed of the Lord will return.
> They will enter Zion with singing; everlasting joy
> will crown their heads.
> Gladness and joy will overtake them, and sorrow
> and sighing will flee away.
>
> I, even I, am he who comforts you (Is. 51:11-12).

Jesus wants to heal our wounds and bring us joy. This blessing of joy from the Father is biblical.

PLAY "WEDDING"

Sometimes we aren't sure about joy — is there such a thing as too much? Should we be stern and disciplined instead? Jesus addresses those in His generation who weren't sure what to believe.

> To what can I compare this generation? They are like children sitting in the marketplaces and calling out to others: "We played the flute for you, and you did not dance; we sang a dirge, and you did not mourn" (Matt. 11:16-17).

These children played funeral, but their friends wouldn't cry. They played wedding, but their friends wouldn't dance and be happy.

> For John came neither eating nor drinking, and they say, "He has a demon." The Son of Man came eating and drinking, and they say, "Here is a glutton and a drunkard, a friend of tax collectors and 'sinners.'" But wisdom is proved right by her actions (vv. 18-19).

I want you to understand what Jesus was telling them. John the Baptist gave them a serious, no-nonsense message of repentance — "turn or burn." But they said, "No, too strict. We want something a little more to our taste, something a little more balanced. We don't want something that serious."

Jesus then came with joy — eating, drinking, healing, feeding and celebrating with them. Yet they called Jesus a glutton and a wine-drinker, a friend of publicans, harlots, sinners and tax collectors. Why do you think they called Him that? Because He was different from all the other religious people of His day. He was out meeting people and enjoying their social gatherings — their weddings and feasts. He was a part of their lives and a member of their culture. Jesus was full of life. Jesus enjoyed people.

But what did the religious people say? "No, not serious enough. Too frivolous. This is not taking the things of God seriously. There is too much happiness here, too much laughter. I want something a little more balanced, a little more middle-of-the-road."

The religious people didn't want what John the Baptist offered *or* what Jesus offered. Some wanted then, just as some want now, the kind of religion that suits them instead of what God wants for them.

Isn't it interesting that the kingdom was offered in two extremes — John as a funeral and Jesus as a wedding? Jesus doesn't offer us a comfortable, middle-of-the-road type of Christianity. What He offers is not really socially acceptable; in fact, it is often a stumbling block to some people. Not everybody is going to like it, and many will not like it whether it's a funeral or a wedding. The church is often caught in this same dilemma.

Well, I believe that the church has played funeral long enough. It is time we played wedding for a while. Let the joy and laughter flow along with all the excitement of the gospel of life.

Dick Schroeder, a campus minister at Montana State University, came to Toronto in January 1995 with some staff members. He described his week with us as "a week in heaven." On his last day here the Holy Spirit came on him with visible shaking. The Lord reminded him of the scripture in which the mother of James and John went to Jesus to ask if her sons could sit at His right hand and His left hand in the kingdom (Matt. 20:20-23). Jesus then asked them if they could drink the cup that He was going to drink. They said they could. Dick writes:

> The Lord was asking me the same question, "Dick, are you willing to drink the cup that I have for you?"
>
> I realized that there is a cost to all of this. There may be a loss of reputation, a great chance of being misunderstood in this whole renewal movement. The Lord may ask us to do things that are out of the ordinary and unusual. I thought about it and said, "Yes, Lord, I will drink the cup."
>
> In my mind, I saw the Lord giving me a cup, and I assumed that the cup would have something bitter in it like vinegar — it would be a tough one to drink because it was going to be a cup of suffering and misunderstanding. As Jesus gave me the cup, I looked back at Him. There was a twinkle in His eye. I looked into the cup. Instead of being vinegar, it was a cup of joy! An eruption of laughter came forth from my innermost being. I fell back and laughed and laughed. I shouted, "It's a cup of joy! Hallelujah! It's a cup of joy!"

Dick remembered that the Bible says, "for the joy that was set before Him [He] endured the cross, despising the shame, and has sat down at the right hand of the throne of God" (Heb. 12:2, NKJV). Dick says he knows there is a cost to it; God is going to require things of us. "But," Dick knows now, "He is giving us His joy."

LET THE PARTY BEGIN

Take a fresh look at the story of the prodigal son. This son demanded his inheritance from his father, then he went to a distant country and squandered it. He ended up destitute, feeding pigs and wishing he could eat what the pigs were eating. But he wised up and said to himself:

> How many of my father's hired men have food to spare, and here I am starving to death! I will set out and go back to my father and say to him: Father, I have sinned against heaven and against you. I am no longer worthy to be called your son; make me like one of your hired men. So he got up and went to his father (Luke 15:17-20).

Now his father must have been looking for his son's return every day, because when his son was still a long way off, he saw him, was filled with compassion and ran to meet him. The son confessed his folly, and his father responded:

> "Quick! Bring the best robe and put it on him. Put a ring on his finger and sandals on his feet. Bring the fattened calf and kill it. Let's have a feast and celebrate. For this son of mine was dead and is alive again; he was lost and is found." So they began to celebrate (vv. 22-24).

Meanwhile, the older son was in the field working. When he found out about this celebration, he was angry. He told his father:

> Look! All these years I've been slaving for you and never disobeyed your orders. Yet you never gave me even a young goat so I could celebrate with my friends. But when this son of yours who has squandered your property with prostitutes comes home, you kill the fattened calf for him!
>
> "My son," the father said, "you are always with me, and everything I have is yours. But we had to

51

celebrate and be glad, because this brother of yours was dead and is alive again; he was lost and is found" (vv. 29-32).

This is such a profound story. The older son would not join in, even though the father pleaded with him. The older brother did not like parties. The younger brother liked them, but what a surprise to learn that the very best party of all was back home all along. Sin is forgiven, shame is removed; only love, acceptance and great joy are flowing.

The older son did not understand that everything in the father's house was his. He could have had a party any time he wanted to. *It was just that he did not want to.* He never did realize that everything of the father's was now his. He thought pleasing his father was the same as working for him. Yet the father was longing for relationship.

The older brother was content to "play funeral" while the father threw a party for the younger son. I'm glad that the younger son was first met by the father and not the older brother.

You may be like the older brother. I believe that there is a little of the older brother in all of us. Realize that the Father will share everything He has with you. You can have a party any time you want. Everything the Father has is yours.

Reverend Margaret Knight and her husband, George, from Chorleywood, U.K., came to our meetings in June 1994. Before they returned to Britain, they left us a note. The Reverend Margaret said this about her Christian walk:

> I had been like the eldest son who was obedient and dutiful. I was dutiful, facilitating others' celebrating, but glancing in while continuing to go about my duties.

Then Reverend Margaret said she decided to enter into the party at our church. Her heart cry for intimacy with the Father was answered, she says, adding this final statement of joy: "Whoopee!"

The prodigal son found out that the very best party of all was right there in his father's house. That is what we are finding out, isn't it? The very best party of all is right here in the Father's house. That is why in Isaiah God describes the party saying, "Come, buy wine and milk without money and without cost...Your soul will delight in the richest of fare" (55:1-2).

The Holy Spirit is so excited because a harvest of lost sons and daughters is coming in. Some older brothers are offended, but we must celebrate. This is a time of dress rehearsal as the church gets ready for thousands of prodigals — the poor, the crippled, the blind, the lame and the oppressed — who will return to their Father's house.

Jonathan Bernis, director of Hear O' Israel Ministries, is a Messianic Jew who now lives in St. Petersburg of the former Soviet Union. He is holding meetings all over Russia in which thousands of Soviet Jews are accepting Jesus as Messiah. Imagine the great joy in the Father's heart as these wayward or lost sons of Israel come "home."

> There is rejoicing in the presence of the angels of God over one sinner who repents (Luke 15:10).

This is what the joy and laughter is all about. The Father is excited and pleased, and the Holy Spirit is pouring this joy out on the church. We do well to remember that it is the Father's idea to celebrate (Luke 15:23). None of this is birthed in the will of man.

Let the Lord fill you with His joy. It is a sign of the Father's presence.

In Your presence is fullness of joy; At Your right hand are pleasures forevermore (Ps. 16:11, NKJV).

It is His presence that brings us joy. The Holy Spirit is God's presence with us. That's why the best party, the best celebration, the most joy is in our Father's house. Will you join in?❂

PART II

CHARACTERISTICS OF THE RENEWAL

CHAPTER 4

EVALUATING THIS MOVE OF GOD

Many people have asked me what led to this outpouring of the Father's blessing. They want to know, Why Toronto? Why us? That's something I'd like to know, too.

A pastor from British Columbia told me that after he heard about the renewal in our church, he pondered visiting us but thought, "Why do I have to go somewhere for revival? Can't God revive us right where we are?" He said the Lord came back with, "Why Azusa Street? Why Angelus Temple? Why Wales? Why not Toronto?"

Obviously, it is a sovereign work of God. We take absolutely no credit for praying this down or deserving it in any way. Let me explain how it came about.

THE BEGINNINGS OF THIS RENEWAL

Carol and I had run dry on ministering in the way we had been. We had a significant "hospital" in our church — people with whom we spent a lot of time counseling and working on inner healing and deliverance. People were maturing and changing. It was wonderful, but it took two or three years for people to become relatively free inside.

We always saw something else that needed to be done. Our focus was on the people, the troubles and the healings needed instead of the Lord. To us, it became as though the devil was too big and the Lord was too small. Our solutions for helping people centered around dealing with the darkness, trying to cast the demons out and heal life's hurts instead of receiving more of the Holy Spirit's presence and power as a main emphasis.

In the fall of 1992, Carol and I went to a meeting in Toronto conducted by Benny Hinn, who is originally from Toronto and has been a friend of mine for twenty years. Benny loves Jesus more than anyone I know and is powerfully used by the Holy Spirit. During this meeting we were jarred into remembering that we truly have a big God who is able to save a thousand people in a night and heal the wheelchair-bound and dozens of seriously ill people.

We purposed in our hearts that we must have more of the anointing, so we began to seek God in a fresh new way. We invited several guest speakers to our church. It didn't matter what their denominational background was. If I heard they were anointed by the Spirit and used by God, I wanted them to come because maybe we could learn something from them. The Bible encourages us to desire spiritual gifts (1 Cor. 14:1), and that is what we did.

In October 1992, Carol and I started giving our entire mornings to the Lord, spending time worshiping, reading, praying and being with Him. For a year and a half we did this, and we fell in love with Jesus all over again.

Intimacy with Jesus is what we signed up for. I did not go into ministry so I could be the CEO of a religious organization, but that was what happened — we had overwhelming administrative loads and no time either to be with people or to be with God. I believe this happens to many pastors and leaders.

We heard about the revival in Argentina, so we traveled there in November 1993, hoping God's anointing would rub off on us somehow. We were powerfully touched in meetings led by Claudio Freidzon, a leader in the Assemblies of God in Argentina.

Claudio prayed for Carol and me. I fell down, then started analyzing the event as I usually did. "Lord, was this really You? Or did I just fall because I want You so badly?" Carol receives from God so easily, but I have always had a difficult time.

After I stood up, Claudio came over to me and said, "Do you want the anointing?"

"Oh yes, I want it all right," I answered.

"Then take it!" He slapped my outstretched hands.

"I will. I will take it," I said.

Something clicked in my heart at that moment. It was as though I heard the Lord say, "For goodness sake, will you take this? Take it, it's yours." And I received by faith.

We came back from Argentina with a great expectation that God would do something new in our church.

We had a taste of what the Lord had planned for us during our New Year's Eve service as we brought in 1994. People were prayed for and powerfully touched by God. They were lying all over the floor by the time the meeting ended. We thought, "This is wonderful, Lord. Every now and then You move in power." But we did not think in terms of sustaining this blessing.

We invited Randy Clark, a casual friend and pastor of the Vineyard Christian Fellowship in St. Louis, Missouri, to speak because we heard that people were being touched powerfully by God when he ministered. We hoped that this anointing would follow him to our church.

Yet Randy and I were in fear and trembling, hoping God would show up in power, but uncertain about what would happen. We were not exactly full of faith — but God was faithful anyway.

On January 20, 1994, the Father's blessing fell on the 120 people attending that Thursday night meeting in our church. Randy gave his testimony, and ministry time began. People fell all over the floor under the power of the Holy Spirit, laughing and crying. We had to stack up all the chairs to make room for everyone. Some people even had to be carried out.

Before Randy and his team came, they prayed. The Lord gave them a vision of a map with a fire breaking out in Toronto then burning up the whole map. God fulfilled this vision. Within days, the word spread that God was visiting us powerfully. But this outpouring didn't look like we thought it would.

We had been praying for God to move, and our assumption was that we would see more people saved and healed, along with the excitement that these would generate. It never occurred to us that God would throw a massive party where people would laugh, roll, cry and become so empowered that emotional hurts from childhood were just lifted off them. The phenomena may be strange, but the fruit this is producing is extremely good.

OUR RENEWAL SERVICES

Let me tell you what our renewal services are like. Six nights a week we start at 7:30 P.M. and worship for about forty-five minutes, then we welcome visitors. We like to see how many people are here for the first time, how many pastors and leaders have come and where everyone is from. We then interview people who wish to testify to what God has done since they've arrived. After an offering and announcements, the Word is preached for about thirty to forty-five minutes.

We always give an invitation for people to receive Christ. We ask for people who want to be born again, and we invite prodigals who want to return to Christ. Five to ten, or even up to thirty to forty people, make commitments or recommitments every night. Most of them are not even from our area. I can hardly believe that people who are not ready to meet God, who are not saved or who are severely backslidden would come to these meetings. But they do, and God meets them.

After that comes the prayer and ministry time. First people come for prayer related to the message. If the message was on unforgiveness, for instance, we invite people who are struggling with unforgiveness to come. After this, anyone may come for prayer, and our ministry teams will pray for them. We ask that people line up in an orderly manner in the back of the auditorium and wait on the Lord in prayer while waiting for the laying on of hands.

Some of our ministry team people have to go to their jobs in the morning, so they usually leave around 11:00 or 11:30 P.M. Others stay until well after midnight, and the doors aren't usually shut until after 1:00 A.M.

We are still a "hospital," but now God is truly the Great Physician. We are seeing people come as children with their hearts open for prayer. As they are touched by God, they are suddenly more loving than they have ever been. They have a fresh revelation of how much God loves them. When that truth hits the heart, what a difference it makes!

So how should we correctly evaluate what we see? Let's

assess this current move of God according to three criteria:
The Word of God, church history and the fruit. Let's look at
each of these.

IS IT SCRIPTURAL?

These questions need to be asked when evaluating a
spiritual experience: Is this in the Word of God? Is something similar in the Word? Is this prohibited by the Word of
God? Is it within the character of God as revealed through
the Bible?

When we ask if something is biblical, we're really asking if
it's from God, aren't we? We don't want to be deceived, and
we have been given the Bible to show us who God is, what
He is like and what kinds of things He does. So we evaluate
things according to the Bible, as we should. Yet as we see
the Spirit of God doing more and more, we may see some
things that no chapter and verse in the Bible specifically
describes. Why?

God did not intend to describe every act He would ever
do in the Bible. John said at the end of his Gospel:

> Jesus did many other things as well. If every one
> of them were written down, I suppose that even
> the whole world would not have room for the
> books that would be written (21:25).

What we need to watch for is God's character, His ways.
How much better to know His ways than His acts! David
asked of God:

> Show me your ways, O Lord, teach me your paths
> (Ps. 25:4).

Just as you know the ways of your spouse or your parents or your children, we need to know the ways of God. If

someone tells you that your spouse did something or other, you know immediately whether that sounds like something he or she would do. You cannot know every action your spouse takes, but as you get to know your spouse better and better, you can know his or her ways. You will then be able to know if something is out of character or not.

The Bible is a record of people's *experiences* with God. Theology is the reflection on these experiences. The theology that Scripture reveals and establishes is essential. But we also need personal experiences with God, just as the people in the Bible had.

Every manifestation of the Spirit, every phenomenon we accept as from God must conform to God's character and His ways. Throughout this book you will find many biblical references that associate a scripture with what we see happening. This is critical; the Bible keeps us from falling into error. I'm convinced the bulk of what we are seeing in this current renewal is from God.

HAS THIS HAPPENED BEFORE IN CHURCH HISTORY?

The second criteria we use to evaluate this move of God is to compare it with church history. What has happened in previous moves of the Spirit? What did they look like? What were the results then? What did those involved conclude?

When God started visiting us powerfully, I did not have any idea that the Holy Spirit's presence could cause such an uproar, and that people would get so excited and fall, shout or roll on the floor. I didn't have a doctrine for that; I didn't understand its history or purpose.

When we read about revivals in church history, we tend to skip over the manifestations of the Spirit and go straight to the large number of people coming to Christ or being healed supernaturally by God's power. We skip over the means — the way God brought people to Christ — and study the end — the number of people saved. But throughout church history, revivals saw the Holy Spirit moving in ways similar to how He is moving here and now.

Richard Riss, an author and friend of mine who is a candidate for a doctorate in church history, has done extensive research into revivals throughout church history. He documents sixty-two different revivals since the 1200s. Many of these had similar manifestations: falling, shaking, visions, trances, and to a lesser degree, laughing and "drunkenness" in the Spirit.

In Jonathan Edwards' day, 250 years ago, the people being moved by the Holy Spirit were accused of being disorderly. Dr. Guy Chevreau, a great friend who has a doctorate in historical theology from Wycliffe College, University of Toronto, has written an excellent book, Catch the Fire, which includes the account of the revival Edwards experienced. We know that revival as The Great Awakening, but then it was called The Great Clamour.[1] Some people hated it.

However, Jonathan Edwards' wife, who was a melancholy woman — godly, but very introverted, nervous and frail — experienced what we would call being drunk in the Spirit for at least seventeen days. After that they stopped documenting. It could have gone on longer; we do not know.

A typical incident during these days was this one:

> These words THE COMFORTER IS COME were accompanied to my soul with such conscious certainty, and such intense joy, that immediately it took away my strength, and I was falling to the floor; when some of those who were near me caught me and held me up.[2]

On the seventeenth day, Mrs. Edwards testified:

> I felt such intense love to Christ, and so much delight in praising Him, that I could hardly forbear

leaping from my chair and singing aloud for joy
and exultation. I continued thus extraordinarily
moved [for two and a half hours].[3]

Several years earlier George Whitefield, the great
Methodist revivalist in the 1700s, was barred from preaching
in any Congregational Church during his second preaching
tour to New England. Why? Because of the seemingly disorderly uproar that accompanied his meetings. Whitefield is
one of the heroes of the faith, a great evangelist. When he
preached, people fell, they laughed, they rolled, they
shouted. They had manifestations similar to those we see,
and a lot of folk did not understand. People said, "This cannot be God because it is not decent and in order."

Bill DeArteaga shows in his book *Quenching the Spirit*
that, throughout church history, every time there is a move
of the Holy Spirit some people come against it. It upsets
their traditions, it moves them out of their comfort zones, it
takes away their jobs or positions. So people find themselves fighting against the move of God, much like the
Pharisees did against Jesus Himself.

Sometimes this pharisaical religious spirit rises up so
powerfully that the move of God is eventually argued out of
existence (1 Thess. 5:19). When the Holy Spirit is quenched
in the church, we are left with just traditions and doctrines,
aren't we? And traditions and doctrines alone don't bring
the good news to the world.

Jonathan Edwards' critics were saying, "If all this is God,
as you say, then why is all this garbage and debris happening
over here?" Now, that is a valid question, isn't it? Edwards'
reply was classic: "It is probable that many of those who are
thus waiting, know not for what they are waiting. If they
wait to see a work of God without difficulties and stumbling blocks, it will be like the fool's waiting at the riverside
to have the water all run by."[4]

We have to look at the main body of the movement, at the thousands of people who have been blessed, not at the few who have missed it for whatever reason. We don't think less of salvation because some lose their relationship with Christ. We don't throw out the Bible because some of the cults have wrongly interpreted it. Why abandon revival because a few folks misinterpret manifestations?

Our brief look points to the fact that church history confirms our experiences. However, for a thorough examination of this subject, I recommend Guy Chevreau's *Catch the Fire* and Patrick Dixon's *Signs of Revival*.

THE FRUIT OF THIS RENEWAL

The fruit produced in a person's life is the third way to evaluate a spiritual experience. I often ask people, "Do you think it was Jesus? Was it the Holy Spirit? What has happened in you?" These same questions were asked to a man God touched almost two thousand years ago.

One Sabbath, Jesus healed a man who was born blind. The religious leaders complained saying, "This man is not from God, for he does not keep the Sabbath" (John 9:16). They asked the formerly blind man who healed him and what he thought about the Man who did this work — yet they rejected his response. But the man who had been healed explained to the leaders that this good fruit was from God.

> We know that God does not listen to sinners. He listens to the godly man who does his will. Nobody has ever heard of opening the eyes of a man born blind. If this man were not from God, he could do nothing (vv. 31-33).

The man born blind summed up his encounter with Jesus in these simple, childlike words: "One thing I do know. I was blind but now I see!" (v. 25). He knew the fruit was good.

Throughout this book you will read testimonies of the results of this renewal in people's lives. People typically tell me that they are more in love with Jesus, and they know in their hearts how much He loves them. They have a renewed hunger for the Word, and they have a broken heart for the lost. Their prayer life is more vital than ever. They are now looking for ways to serve Him.

As this move of the Spirit spreads around the world, sooner or later you will talk to someone who has been touched by it. Tens of thousands now have a story to tell, often with a similar theme: "I don't understand why I shook, fell, laughed, cried, rolled, jerked or whatever. But one thing I know, I used to be fearful; I used to be crippled inside; I used to be ineffective as a Christian; I used to have to use all my energy to keep my emotional strength up just to live another day; I used to be bound by hurts and fears. But now I am free, because the Spirit of God came to me and released me."

Why are people offended by what the Holy Spirit does? Why were they offended with Jesus' ministry? Because God is always doing something different from what people expect Him to do. Even John the Baptist began to wonder if Jesus was the one. Perhaps things were not going as John expected. From jail, he sent his disciples to ask Jesus if He was the Christ.

Jesus told them to tell John about the fruit — the lame walking, the dead being raised. And as if to say, "Oh, by the way," He added: "Blessed is he who is not offended because of Me" (Luke 7:23, NKJV). By this He encouraged people to judge the impact and not be offended by the means.

For months and months now, we have been saying, "Oh, Holy Spirit, would You please come and give Your people more?" Then He comes, and people do the funniest things which we might say are not necessarily decent and in order. But when they get up, they are full of joy, their hearts are healed and they are in love with Jesus. The fruit is wonderful.

As an introduction to the results of this renewal and the wonderful testimonies you will read about in this book, let me introduce you to Bill Subritzky. I met Bill in the early nineties in conferences in England and Hungary at which he was the keynote speaker. He is a widely known and very well respected Anglican evangelist and lawyer. I was pleasantly surprised to see him and his wife, Pat, at our meetings in Auckland, New Zealand, in June 1995. He was powerfully touched by God.

The next day, on his national radio program, he told the nation of New Zealand what he had experienced. It impacted a lot of people. It is so thrilling to see God come in sovereign power and so completely bless a man of his stature and reputation in the body of Christ. Carol and I knew that not only were he and his family profoundly impacted, but his own ministry would have a greater anointing to see the kingdom come in greater power to win the lost for Christ.

Here is Bill's story in his own words.

> Prior to John and Carol Arnott's visit to New Zealand, I had received many letters and faxes from around the world asking for my view on "the Toronto blessing." I refused to make any comment until I had personally observed what was happening. So I went to John and Carol Arnott's meeting with a completely open mind. I told the Lord that I would receive anything He had for me.
>
> At the first session, I sensed that the power of God was present as John spoke in his very calm,

67

yet anointed, way. At the conclusion of the meeting they prayed for people. As Carol approached me, laid hands upon me and began to pray, I sensed the power of God falling on me in a mighty way. I must have rested in the Spirit for nearly two hours, with both Carol and others praying for me. Toward the end of this time I suddenly felt a surge of joy which flowed up from my belly into my mouth, and I laughed heartily for probably thirty minutes. I knew the real joy and peace of the Lord.

During my twenty-four years of ministry, I have conducted crusades in Africa, South America, North America, Europe and around the Pacific basin. It has been my privilege to see tens of thousands of people fall under the power of the Holy Spirit in these crusades. Yet in all of these years, I had never fallen under the power of the Holy Spirit myself.

Yet when I was asked to testify on the platform the next morning, I was able to get only part of my testimony out before the power of God fell on me again. I spent the next two hours lying on the platform. That night the same thing happened. The Lord gave me the words, "And they say this is not of Me." I barely uttered them before deep laughter came from within me, and again I spent the next two hours resting in the Spirit.

The effect on me has been dramatic. While I was on the floor the Lord said to me very clearly, "You have given out for years, now I am giving in to you." As an evangelist, I have prayed for tens of thousands of people in all sorts of situations — and I realize now just how weary I was. The scripture in Acts 3:19 about "times of refreshing may come from the presence of the Lord" (NKJV) has become a tremendous reality for me. I am being continually refreshed with the presence of the Lord.

There remains therefore a rest for the people of God. For he who has entered His rest has himself also ceased from his works as God did from His (Heb. 4:9-10, NKJV).

I never fully understood that scripture before, but now I have entered God's rest. The peace of God has filled me completely. I am much more relaxed in the Spirit, and I can hear the voice of the Lord more clearly. I have a greater thirst for God, and I have become a gentler person.

When I was born again, I had never seen the grass so green, the trees so beautiful or heard the birds sing so wonderfully. The morning after I had received this refreshing, I felt exactly the same way. As I looked around me I could not get over the vividness of color. Everything seemed to take on new life.

I now sense a new vitality and freshness in my preaching. I have ceased working in the flesh and have relied totally upon the Holy Spirit. Whereas in the past I was worn out after three nights of crusades, I have been able to conduct four major crusades with thousands of people present, plus conduct major seminars.

My evangelistic messages have taken on a new dimension, and the anointing has increased dramatically. I have been privileged to see many people mightily touched under the anointing of the Holy Spirit as I have prayed for them.

Two weeks after this experience I was in Papua New Guinea conducting crusades, and as I prayed for fifteen leaders, these reserved people all fell under the power of the Holy Spirit. Everybody except one person immediately received the gift of laughter. They were on the floor for several hours and had to be stirred in time for the crusade. It was quite apparent from the expressions on their faces that they had a mighty touch from God.

I have always believed that men should not cry. However, since I have had this experience, I have found that often as the power of the Holy Spirit comes upon me, I have wanted to weep. I know that a great cleansing has been taking place within me.

The Lord has also dealt with deep things in my life. When I was eight years of age, my five-year-old brother died. My mother never got over his death. For the next fourteen years she grieved until she herself died. However, all her grief was suppressed, and I was always taught to suppress my grief and my feelings. God has given me a mighty healing in my spirit and that grief has been replaced by His joy.

The Word of God has become even more vital and real to me. As I read the Word I feel I am being bathed and refreshed. I have a greater thirst for God and know His peace in a special way. The reality of His presence is quite overwhelming.

OPEN UP TO GOD

As you read on, please evaluate everything by Scripture, church history and the fruit. I am confident that by the end of the book you will be ready and willing to open yourself up to the Lord and receive everything God has for you.☻

DECENTLY AND IN ORDER

O ur church was praying for revival, just as many of yours are. We realize now we forgot to ask what revival would look like. We thought God would come and somehow, quietly and reverently, large numbers of people would be converted and healed. The church would grow, and there would be joy, but everything would be somewhat subdued at the level we were used to and comfortable with.

But when the Spirit of God came, it was like an explosion. We saw people literally being knocked off their feet by the

Spirit of God — when no one else was near them. Others shook and jerked. Some danced, some laughed. Some lay on the floor as if dead for hours. People cried and shouted.

Lives were dramatically transformed. A young man named Steve who was always on the fringe of church life began to shake and prophesy and is now a vibrant witness for Jesus. And his story of renewal is repeated over and over in the lives of many who have visited our church.

We were so dry and desperate, we were willing to accept what God was doing in fear and trembling. Now that we understand how good and sweet the experience of the Holy Spirit is, we love it and say, "More, Lord."

WELCOMING THE HOLY SPIRIT

The atmosphere in our church services is electric — charged with the presence of God. At times, the intensity of the manifestations of the Holy Spirit in our meetings is frankly shocking. Occasionally, we found ourselves having to speak over the noise of people laughing, groaning or crying out, though usually things are quiet during the preaching of the Word.

When all of this started happening in our church, there was a great temptation to try to keep things "tidy." I wondered how all this fit in with 1 Corinthians 14:40.

Let all things be done decently and in order (KJV).

Were we "decent and in order"? We wanted everything to be in accordance with this scripture. The church needs to function in an orderly way so the body of Christ is edified and the people are blessed, and so there is not mass confusion. Yet we have seen times when the Holy Spirit has come on everyone so strongly that He has almost taken over entirely. I have felt that I might as well sit down and let the Lord take it because such power and blessing was being poured down on the people.

The Holy Spirit reserves the right to fall upon the people, even during the preaching of the Word. He did this to Peter in Cornelius' house (Acts 10:44).

Because of our fears or pride, we want to be in charge. Pastors and leaders are prone to try to be in control of what happens in their churches. They don't like somebody coming along and rocking their boat — even if it's God doing the rocking.

Because we're human, sometimes things are done inappropriately, and we need the wisdom of God to integrate renewal into our communities and churches. But the real question is this: Who is in control? I think Jesus wants His church back. He wants to take control.

Stephan Witt, pastor of Rothesay Vineyard Christian Fellowship in New Brunswick, Canada, talks about this very thing. While on a prayer walk during a sabbatical in North Carolina, Stephan felt God ask, "Who is the priority in your church, the Holy Spirit or people?" It was an appropriate question because for the past two years, Stephan had been working on making the church "user friendly" and "seeker sensitive" focusing on welcoming the people more than welcoming God.

Their church is in a new building in a visible location. Stephan explains:

> We had a large billboard announcing our services. We had coffee in the lobby, proper signs directing visitors to appropriate destinations. Visitors received a handwritten letter from the pastor, visits and a free worship tape just for "being with us today." A visitor was assured of an abbreviated, but quality worship time followed by a culturally relevant message that would get them back on the road again before they started feeling uncomfortable.

So when God asked him who had priority in his church, Stephan was deeply challenged. When he responded that he wanted the Holy Spirit to be the priority, God replied, "Then make the church a place where I feel welcome."

Stephan confesses that their church spent much effort in making the visitor feel welcome, but had not considered how they might make the Spirit feel at home. "Just when we thought it was safe to bring someone to church — dum, dum...dum, dum — like the shark in *Jaws,* the Holy Spirit shows up!"

This is a wonderful challenge for all of us to answer. Are we really welcoming the Holy Spirit into our lives, individually and as a body? Are we welcoming what is occurring — that which the book of Acts calls "times of refreshing"? (3:19). During these times the Lord comes sovereignly and does things that none of us have had any experience in or even seen before. But similar phenomena are recorded in church history.

So the question really is, Whose understanding of "decently and in order" should we use — yours, ours or God's? Let's see what God's definition is — and isn't — by looking at our assumptions about how God moves.

FALSE ASSUMPTION #1: I HAVE TO UNDERSTAND IT OR IT IS NOT GOD

Sometimes God does things that are hard to understand. Some of the phenomena we are seeing in this renewal are hard to understand. Yet the experiences of the people in the Bible show us that when it is God moving, and strange or unusual things happen, there is good fruit and people are blessed.

God told Abraham to sacrifice his son Isaac, the son God had miraculously given him (Gen. 22). Abraham must not have understood why, but he followed God anyway. How many wives would have said to Abraham, "Well, OK, Honey, whatever you think the Lord is saying." No, they would have been on the phone, dialing 911. "Someone get over here quick — my husband has flipped out. He is a religious fanatic!"

We know now that God provided a ram to sacrifice instead of Isaac, but Abraham didn't know that would happen. That is why the Lord says that Abraham believed God and it was counted to him as righteousness (Rom. 4:3). He trusted God about something he couldn't understand. Issac was an amazing type of Christ and the Father offering Him for mankind. It makes perfect sense, looking back over the perspective of time, with Isaac as a type of Jesus and Abraham as a type of God the Father.

Consider again the healing of the blind man recorded in John 9. Jesus spit on the ground, made mud and spread it on the blind man's eyes. He told the man to go and wash, and the man came back able to see. Why didn't Jesus simply lay hands on the man, or anoint him with oil? Why this bizarre practice of spit and mud and washing? We are left to wonder!

We have a tendency to skip over these events because they happened long ago and far away. We don't stop to think about what they would look like today. But what if something similar happened in your church next week? Would you recognize it as God if it really was?

We have the same God today people did then — the God of the whole Bible. This is the God we need to welcome into our hearts, lives and church services. This is the God who is continually doing new things, the God of variety.

P. J. Hanley, an elder from a church in New York, described his first meeting at our church, which he came to rather skeptically.

It was like walking into a heavenly insane asylum.
People were laughing uncontrollably, weeping

uncontrollably, shaking uncontrollably, bounding, roaring, flopping...bodies on the floor, all being powerfully impacted by the Holy Spirit. The presence of God was so wonderful and the worship was unlike anything I have ever experienced. Although there was still some resistance in me (because of the weirdness of it all), I knew that God was doing something wonderful in His people.

The testimonies were so powerful. Whole lives and churches were transformed. And the ministry of the Word was so pure and sharp that it cut my soul like a knife. I began to really open myself to the Lord and seek Him that He would fill me up as He was obviously doing with others.

What would have happened if Mr. Hanley had decided not to pursue this because he didn't understand it? He pushed through his discomfort and lack of mental understanding and received from God.

> The man without the Spirit does not accept the things that come from the Spirit of God, for they are foolishness to him, and he cannot understand them, because they are spiritually discerned (1 Cor. 2:14).

This is not to say that people who do not accept this renewal do not have the Spirit — absolutely not. But it does show us that our natural minds, our rational beings, are never going to completely understand the things of the Spirit of God. They will look foolish. God chooses the foolish things to shame to wise, so no one can boast before Him (1 Cor. 1:27-31).

This new move of God is in line with the Word and with church history. It produces good fruit — Jesus is glorified. Given all that, it seems less important that we cannot understand with our minds all the ways God chooses to do by the Spirit.

FALSE ASSUMPTION #2: THE HOLY SPIRIT WILL NEVER DO ANYTHING AGAINST MY WILL

The people who come to our church want to receive from God. Many eventually say, "Whatever You want, God." Their hearts are open to what God has for them, but sometimes what He does seems "against their will" since they are not making their bodies shake or fall — yet it happens. And sometimes God sovereignly overrules a person's will — because He's God!

The apostle Peter experienced something from God that went against his will.

> Peter went up on the roof to pray. He became hungry and wanted something to eat, and while the meal was being prepared, he fell into a trance (Acts 10:9-10).

Now we are talking about Peter, the apostle of Jesus Christ, falling into a trance. What does that mean? It means, he fell into a trance! Was it Peter's will to fall into a trance? No, but it was God's will. No doubt he cooperated.

Peter then had this glorious vision of a sheet being lowered with all kinds of unclean animals in it. Peter was astounded. The God of the Bible, the God of Abraham, Isaac and Jacob, was telling him to do something that is contrary to Scripture as he understood it, to eat unclean food — which interpreted meant to preach to the gentiles and allow them to enter the kingdom. Now that is a very puzzling thing, but it is one of the ways of God. God was doing a new thing, and He went against Peter's will and beliefs to show it to him.

Zechariah also discovered that God can act against a

77

man's will. He was a priest who went into the temple of the Lord to do his term of service. Suddenly an angel came to him and told him that he and his wife would have a son.

Zechariah questioned the angel's words. He was probably thinking, "This is pretty unlikely, angel. We are getting old and have no children, so how is this going to happen?" The angel responded by taking away Zechariah's ability to speak until "the day this happens" (Luke 1:20). This was obviously done against Zechariah's will, yet it was from God.

What if this happened to a senior couple in your church today? Are you going to explain to the rest of his family that he thinks he has seen and heard from an angel of God, yet he cannot talk? Or are you going to say, "This can't be from God because it goes against this dear old man's will"? Remember, Zechariah was unable to speak for nine months!

These are manifestations of the Holy Spirit's power. Why would God do things like this? Well, these are the ways of God.

Steven Thauberger, a hearing-impaired man, came to our church because his sister invited him. He was not a believer, so when she told him what was happening, he said, "Yeah, right." He didn't want to be rude, so he came with her.

He became nervous when he saw the dancing and laughing. Then someone came up and asked if he wanted to be prayed for. He said sure. Immediately, he fell down.

He thought to himself, "That was really neat." He got up and asked someone else to pray for him. He fell down again and started tumbling around in circles. "After that," he states emphatically, "I believed."

I asked him why that experience caused him to believe. He replied, "I have no answer for that. I just know. Sometimes I feel His presence...I don't know how to explain it." As he was trying to find a way to describe what happened to him, he started shaking and went down again. When this man fell, it was not something he willed to do; yet it was from God, and he did not resist it.

Let's look in the book of Acts at the story of Ananias and Sapphira. They sold all their property and kept part of the money for themselves instead of giving it all to the church. That was OK, but then Ananias and Sapphira conspired together to lie about it. Peter confronted Ananias about lying to God, and Ananias fell down and died.

The same thing happened to his wife, Sapphira, when Peter questioned her and she lied also.

> At that moment she fell down at his feet and died. Then the young men came in and, finding her dead, carried her out and buried her beside her husband. Great fear seized the whole church and all who heard about these events (Acts: 5:10-11).

Ananias and Sapphira fell under the power of God, too — and against their wills. The difference was, they didn't get up. The power came in judgment. Was this move of the Spirit against their wills? Yes. But was it God? Yes.

If that had happened in your church, what would you say? "Oh, they have gone too far now. Two people died in the service this morning."

So not only did God move in a way that went against Ananias and Sapphira's will, but also His actions brought great fear. Why is it then that people often think they will have no fear in God's presence?

FALSE ASSUMPTION #3: IF IT IS TRULY GOD, I WILL NOT BE AFRAID

Whenever God appeared throughout the Bible, people were told not to be afraid.[1] Why? Because people are afraid when God shows Himself. We sometimes think, "Why am I feeling afraid? I know this is not God because I feel nervous in this meeting." Yet feeling afraid might just be the way you truly know it is God, because every time God showed up in power in the Bible, people were afraid.

Terry Virgo, the international overseer of New Frontiers Churches, wrote to me about his visit to our church. Earlier Carol and I were with him in Brighton, England, in October 1994. At one point he was lying down with one of us at his head and one at his feet, soaking him in the power of God. He was saying, "My whole body is on fire. I have never been this high before. I don't know what to do."

When I asked him later, he said he was afraid and, "My whole body was on fire. I felt that there was a driving hailstorm right in my face." Is it any wonder that he shook a little bit? Is it any wonder he was afraid?

After this and other similar experiences, Terry is now ministering the gospel in a whole new level of power.

God showed up in a powerful vision when Daniel prayed to the Lord about his people, the Israelites, who were in exile in Babylon. The Bible says the men that were with him were terrified.

> As I was standing on the bank of the great river, the Tigris, I looked up and there before me was a man dressed in linen, with a belt of the finest gold around his waist. His body was like chrysolite, his face like lightning, his eyes like flaming torches, his arms and legs like the gleam of burnished bronze, and his voice like the sound of a multitude.
>
> I, Daniel, was the only one who saw the vision; the men with me did not see it, but such terror overwhelmed them that they fled and hid themselves (Dan. 10:4-7).

Why do you suppose the Bible speaks of the fear of God 353 times?[2] Every time God shows up, we read, "Fear not."

Why? Because it scares us to death when God shows up. The men with Daniel did not see what he saw, yet they ran away in terror and hid themselves. Daniel was left alone, gazing at the vision.

> I had no strength left, my face turned deathly pale and I was helpless. Then I heard him speaking, and as I listened to him, I fell into a deep sleep, my face to the ground (vv. 8-9).

Why would God do that when He comes? I don't know. We are not used to God's coming in that kind of power. Someone might have said to Daniel, "You don't look so good. This must not be God. Would God do this? Is this what He calls 'decent and in order'?"

Daniel lay paralyzed on the ground. He describes what happened next:

> A hand touched me and set me trembling on my hands and knees. He said, "Daniel, you who are highly esteemed, consider carefully the words I am about to speak to you, and stand up, for I have now been sent to you." And when he said this to me, I stood up trembling.
> Then he continued, "Do not be afraid, Daniel" (vv. 10-12).

Why was Daniel afraid if it was really God? Because He is an awesome God, a powerful God.

Lillian Boycott of Windsor, Ontario, attended a pastor's conference at our church in July 1994. At a noon meeting, she was up at the front shaking when she got scared and forced herself to stay still. At the meeting that night she was walking back to her chair when she realized she didn't need her cane anymore. The arthritis in her left knee was healed. God's power had moved in her; she felt it and it scared her, but the anointing did its work anyway. I was in contact with her a year later, and she was still walking without her cane.

When God showed up on the mountain, the people of Israel trembled, telling Moses to go talk with God himself, and they would do whatever God told them. However, they wanted to stay at a safe distance (Ex. 19).

Do you remember what God told Moses? "You cannot look on my face and live. I will have to cover you till I pass by, and then I will show you my glory." Moses saw the glory of God as it was going away from him; he did not see the brightness of His face (Ex. 33:19-23).

Even though Moses saw only the back of God, his face was glowing and shining like the sun when he came down from that mountain. He had to be covered with a veil because people could not stand looking at him (Ex. 34:35). It was like, "Please, Moses, cover your face. We cannot take it." That was God's power on him.

We are not talking about some slight thing here. The Holy Spirit of God comes in incredible power. When we first experienced the increase of the Holy Spirit's power, the Lord told us, "I am going easy on you now so that when the real power shows up, you will not be terrified."

Comparatively speaking, we have not really seen anything yet. If we can't participate when the power is low, what are we going to do when the real power shows up? What we see now is just the hors d'oeuvres being served. Realize that God is awesome, and don't be surprised if His power overwhelms you.

FALSE ASSUMPTION #4: GOD IS TIDY AND PROPER

We associate reverence and respect and quiet with God. But if we really look at some of the ways He often moved in the Bible, we will see the exact opposite. When phenomena start happening in a church service, the tendency is to stop them and keep the service tidy and explainable. Why? Because they quickly take us out of our comfort zone. But if we do that, we may be shutting down the Holy Spirit. Did anything happen in the Bible that confirms this idea?

We find in Luke 8 that Jesus crossed a sea, endured a storm and accepted censure and rejection simply to set one man free from the bonds of the devil. But it was a noisy and confusing affair.

This man lived in the tombs, naked and possessed. Broken chains dangled from his wrists. The community was helpless to deal with him, so they completely ignored and shunned him. He was left living among the dead, crying out and cutting himself in the misery and torment of demonic possession.

As soon as Jesus' boat hit the beach, everything exploded. Jesus commanded the evil spirit to come out of the man as he was charging down the hill screaming. Jesus asked, "What is your name?" The man replied, "Legion, for we are many." The demons were ordered out and they begged Christ to let them enter the pigs feeding nearby. The whole herd then rushed down the steep bank into the lake and was drowned (Luke 8:33).

The keepers of the pigs, the herdsman, ran in great fear back to their village. The people came out and begged Jesus to leave. Why? Because they were terrified. This was not a neat and tidy event. Two thousand pigs died, and people were supposed to believe God was in this?

Suppose this happened in your church. It would need to be a country church with some pigs nearby, but think of all the screaming and shouting going on. Jesus, then the man, then the demons, then the pigs and the villagers as well! How could this be God? It's so loud and perplexing.

Had those been your pigs, what would you have thought? You just lost two thousand times, let's say, $250 or so — around a half million dollars just went into the sea. Your community would be split about whether this was God or not, whether this was a good work or not.

But, if you had asked the mother of that young man if she thought this was the work of the Holy Spirit, what do you think she would have said? If you had asked the young man what happened to him, what do you think he would have said? Would he have wondered if everything was done "decently and in order"? No. Instead we read that he was so grateful and awestruck that he asked Jesus if he could go with Him. But he was to go home and tell his family and friends how much God had done for him (vv. 38-39). Jesus wanted him to be a witness to God's work.

Some others, however, will always react negatively, especially when it hits them financially. But that does not mean it is not a work of the Spirit. God works in His order. He is not subject to our rules for tidiness and proper behavior.

Consider the divine rescue of Paul and Silas while in jail at Philippi. They had been stripped and beaten for healing a demonized girl and subsequently starting a riot in the city. At midnight, a violent earthquake struck, shaking the very foundations of the prison. But this was no ordinary earthquake — it was the Holy Spirit visiting the prison and setting all the prisoners free.

The hardened jailer was converted as he cried out in fear, "What must I do to be saved?" (Acts 16:29). His faith did not rest on the wisdom of man, but on the awesome power of God (1 Cor. 2:5). Philippi was shaken that day — physically and spiritually. It was not a neat and tidy event.

When Stephan Witt, the pastor from New Brunswick, and the other leaders in his church returned from services in our church in Toronto, they had a Saturday night debriefing meeting with other leaders in their church. When they prayed, people fell and laughed and experienced God's manifest presence.

Stephan relates thinking, "What if this breaks out tomorrow morning in church?" It concerned him because it appeared chaotic and messy. Stephan continues:

I was wondering what some of our new people would think if they saw our leaders doing what they had done the night before. The explanation for this phenomena is not carried in our visitor's packet. Lord help us if we have to carry people out! I made a very important decision at that time — who cares!

And the results the next day? Stephan told me:

When the dust settled, over one hundred people were doing "carpet time," and the Holy Spirit wasn't finished. We finally concluded the morning meeting at 3:30 in the afternoon, having seen massive laughter, joy, peace, deliverance and such. We immediately called for meetings every night to soak in the presence of the Holy Spirit.

I've discovered that if the simple, humble yet powerful ways of the Holy Spirit offend us, then we will find some logical reason to tidy it up — and pretty soon we will not have to worry about His ways bothering us anymore. I'd rather have the Holy Spirit come on His terms than mine, even if at times I am uncomfortable and do not understand.

Trust God

Here is the bottom line. If you know that God is a God of love and that His heart is for you and not against you, you can come to Him in childlike faith and ask for the fullness of His Spirit, can't you? And if you ask a loving

85

God for more with a right heart and a right motive, what are you going to get? More of Him.

Is that what you want? Then don't allow things you can't quite understand to keep you from being healed and renewed. God is fearsome, awe-inspiring and sometimes perplexing. He doesn't always act within our culturally acceptable parameters of proper and polite behavior. Oh, but when He acts, when He works, don't let anything keep you from entering in.

It can be a fearful thing to totally trust someone. But do you know something? You can totally trust the Holy Spirit. You have a loving Father who has promised to send the Holy Spirit to you. Open your heart to Him. He's faithful. Trust Him. ✪

CHAPTER 6

RECEIVING THE
SPIRIT'S POWER

Carol and I are a study in opposites when it comes to receiving the things of God. As a general rule, when someone prays for me I do not feel anything. Carol, on the other hand, receives very easily.

If you were having a rather bad day and wondered if God were still with you, you could pray for Carol and she would receive wonderfully and probably fall down. You would feel better, knowing that God was still with you and answering prayer.

Whenever Carol and I went to a meeting where the Spirit

of God was really moving — like at a Benny Hinn crusade, a John Wimber meeting or a good prayer meeting — Carol would receive the Spirit, fall down and say, "Oh, what I feel is so wonderful."

I would ask, "Honey, what do you feel?"

"Oh, it's so wonderful," she would say. I would be thrilled for her, yet at the same time I would be aware of my own unfulfilled desire for refreshing. I have previously felt God's presence powerfully at my conversion and my Spirit baptism and on one or two other occasions, but until this renewal, I had not felt His overwhelming nearness for many years.

If I was prayed for and I happened to fall down, I was never sure if I fell because everything happened so fast or because catchers behind me pulled me back. Maybe I had been pushed over or hit so hard on the forehead that I was knocked down, or perhaps I just wanted God so badly that I fell over because that was what was expected of me. I would lie there on the floor thinking to myself, "I don't feel anything, and I don't want to make this up or hype it. I might as well get up right now."

Carol and I went to Rodney Howard-Browne's meeting in Fort Worth when we were visiting our daughters in June 1993. He called for all of the pastors to come forward. Carol was with me, and I was right at the end of the line. A couple hundred of us were all around the front of the church, and Rodney went along praying, "Fill, fill, fill."

While I was standing there I chose not to watch. I was just in God's presence. Rodney came along to me said, "Oh Lord, fill this man, come to this man." He did not push me. I felt he honestly tried to impart the Holy Spirit to me, but I felt nothing. And he went on.

When I opened my eyes, I saw that one other man and I were still standing. That's when a person might think, "Well, I am just not given to this sort of thing."

RECEIVE BY FAITH

All of this caused me to relearn an old lesson: We receive everything from God by faith.

When we pray to receive the Spirit, He will often be very gentle, almost so that one may wonder, "Am I imagining this, or is this really You, Lord?" That is when the step of faith is required. At this point people can resist or submit. This is the time to get out of the boat and walk on the water in childlike trust.

I had to start receiving that way — by faith instead of by feelings. That's how I should have received all along. So after I started exercising my faith, I got to the point where experiencing the manifestations and feelings was not important to me, which is a good place to be. Everybody could fall except me, and I really did not mind. I was receiving the things of God, whether I felt I was or not.

If you are one of those who are frustrated because you don't seem to be feeling much of anything, you must accept this fact: When you ask, you receive the Spirit of God whether you feel anything or not because the things of God are received by faith. The feelings are great, and I love them as much as anybody, but everyone receives by faith. The righteous will live by faith (Gal. 3:11).

I love to tell the story about Jim Robb, a Vineyard pastor from Washington, D.C. He came to our meeting in April 1994 because he wanted to receive the power of the Spirit in a refreshing new way.

Jim stayed three or four days and nothing much happened. He phoned home to say he was staying longer. Twenty-three days later he went home discouraged because his perception was that he did not receive an anointing or refreshing from God. He had felt or manifested nothing.

Sunday came and Jim said to himself, "I will pray for the people anyway, as I always used to do." But when he went into ministry time at church, the Holy Spirit hit like a tidal wave. It was incredible. People were strewn all over the floor — some laughing, some crying. It was so wonderful and totally unexpected by him.

Pastor Robb was now excited. He did not phone or fax me, but got back on an airplane and flew to Toronto to tell me face-to-face that he really had received after all. Because he had persisted in prayer for twenty-one days, God had filled his life. It became obvious when he ministered in his church. To fall, shake a bit or to laugh was not the issue. He had really received by faith.

Let's look at some things that help us receive by faith.

TAKE RISKS

We are called to diligently seek God. We are called to come in humility. We are called to come like a little child, not holding back in fear and not playing it safe. If Peter had played it safe, he never would have stepped out of the boat. You might say, "Well, he sank, didn't he?" Yes, but he walked too, didn't he?

John Wimber says the way to spell faith is R-I-S-K.

If you wanted to find out what it was like to walk on water, you would have had to ask Peter. Why? Because he tried something the others were afraid to do — he got out of that boat.

Press into God by faith — risk saying, "Lord, I want more of You. I want more of the Holy Spirit (Heb. 11:6). I am willing to let You take control."

Michael Szabo of Yorkton, Saskatchewan, wrote me about what happened when God moved this renewal into his church, Dayspring Fellowship. For the first three weeks Michael attended the new Tuesday night services, but he was full of doubt and skepticism. He watched people fall, shake uncontrollably, laugh, weep and "act silly." But he admitted he sensed the presence of God and His Spirit stirring inside.

Within a few weeks Michael allowed people to pray over him, but he still resisted God.

> At last I surrendered to the Lord and fell under the presence of the Holy Spirit. For forty minutes I lay on the carpet, unable to speak or move, yet fully conscious of all that was happening around me. While on the carpet, I began to have visions and eventually saw Jesus extend His arms and hug me. I remember weeping with joy and did not want this time to end. I knew I had been touched by God's loving hand and would never be the same.

Michael took the risk, and now he says, "I must witness at every opportunity and not only walk as a Christian but also speak of His love." What happened to him was God. Both his grown daughters accepted Jesus as Savior at our church in August 1995. Michael is still praising God for this.

BE PERSISTENT

If we want what God has for us today, and more of it, we must be persistent. We must keep pressing in, keep seeking God's face and not allow ourselves to become discouraged if God does not do what we expect. God will honor persevering prayer and the steady pursuit of intimacy with Him.

Elisha set a high value on persistence. He knew he was called to succeed Elijah as prophet, to take on his mantle (1 Kin. 19:19-21). When the time came for Elijah to depart, he tried to put Elisha off. It was a test — how badly did Elisha want more of God? Elijah tells Elisha:

> "Stay here; the Lord has sent me to Bethel." But Elisha said, "As surely as the Lord lives and as you live, I will not leave you." So they went down to Bethel (2 Kin. 2:2).

The prophets at Bethel told Elisha that his master Elijah would be taken from him today. This same thing happened in Jericho, then at the Jordan. Elisha pressed through Elijah's test of "You wait here." I believe he had always been a very obedient young man when he was with Elijah, but not this time. He sensed that this was a test. He was persistent. He pushed through, and he followed Elijah.

When they got to the other side of the Jordan, Elijah asked,

> "Tell me, what can I do for you before I am taken from you?"
> "Let me inherit a double portion of your spirit," Elisha replied (v. 9).

Elisha knew what it meant to be persistent, and he received what he had pressed in for — a double portion of Elijah's anointing. He highly valued the anointing of God, and he pursued it diligently.

Terry Appell was persistent. He is the senior pastor of the Christian Life Centre Mona Vale in Sydney, Australia. He said to his church, "There's got to be more to Christianity than what I'm experiencing." This desperation led to persistence.

When he saw the article in *Charisma* magazine about the Father's blessing here in Toronto, first he called us, then he faxed us — then in desperation he got on a plane and came. A fellow pastor, Jeff Beacham, encouraged him to come, and his persistence paid off.

In our meetings Terry wept and wept and wept. He had grown up in an orphanage where he had been placed when he was two years old, and God took him through his inner pain. He tells us:

> When I thought I'd had enough, God would show me more. He showed me myself as a two-year-old baby, crawling up into my own lap [as an adult]

and accepting myself for the first time. I understand now the pain that children go through. I had shut it up for forty years.

Terry said that when people came to him for counseling he said, "Repent. Next." He just couldn't feel people's pain. "But now," he declared joyfully, "I'm a new man." He described through tears the first thing he planned to do when he got home: "I'm going to take my son in my arms and just love on him."

Terry's persistence paid off.

COME AS A CHILD

In order to receive by faith, we need to come to God in trust and humility, just as children come to their parents.

> At that time the disciples came to Jesus and asked, "Who is the greatest in the kingdom of heaven?" (Matt. 18:1).

That is a good question. Inside, don't we all want to be great in the kingdom of heaven, heroes in godly things, successful?

> He called a little child and had him stand among them. And he said: "I tell you the truth, unless you change and become like little children, you will never enter the kingdom of heaven. Therefore, whoever humbles himself like this child is the greatest in the kingdom of heaven. And whoever welcomes a little child like this in my name welcomes me" (vv. 2-5).

Jesus is saying that unless we change and become like little children, we cannot even enter the kingdom of God.

He places a high value on simplicity and trust.

When was the last time you became like a little child? I don't know about you, but that idea bothers me a bit. You know what kids are like, don't you? If you have children or have been around them, you know that they are often playing when they should be doing their chores or their schoolwork. They love to play around. They don't take life seriously enough.

In this scripture, Jesus is calling us to receive the kingdom like little children. Yes, there is a time to become a man and put away childish things, but we are never to become so sophisticated that we can no longer receive simply from God. Don't get so theological and so full of purpose and strategy and your own agendas that you cannot be like a little child, have fun and be simple, trusting, uncomplicated, open and honest before God.

This is a call to get real and to stop playing religious games. It doesn't matter how good we look on the outside, if on the inside many things are wrong. If you are having marriage problems, if you are having problems with lust, if you are having financial problems, if you are having a problem sleeping — whatever kind of problems you might have — bring them into the open. A little child would come and say, "Mommy, I am having nightmares" or "Daddy, I need your help." We must come as little children.

If you have needs or secrets, get them out into the open — tell some trusted friend. Don't pretend they're not there because people will disapprove. Be vulnerable and open with your needs, just as children are.

A little child would take what the Lord wanted to give even if it was packaged with falling, speaking in tongues or shaking. We can say, "Lord, just come and do what You want to do. I am not going to set the terms. I am not going to set the agenda here." God is going to give you the desire of your heart when you come in childlike faith.

PRESS IN AND TAKE WHAT GOD OFFERS

Most of the things that we receive from the Lord begin in the natural and end in the spiritual. Before you panic about being in the flesh, just think about it.

When you come to worship, you may not always feel like worshiping. But you have learned how to enter in, so during that first or second song, it is 90 percent you and 10 percent God. You make yourself raise your hands, and as you give more of yourself to God, that ratio turns around and eventually becomes 90 percent God as you feel His wonderful presence on you and just 10 percent you. Do you understand?

Reading the Bible is the same way. You might not feel like reading the Bible. When you start it is 90 percent you and 10 percent God. But once you get into it, you get so blessed. The percentage turns around.

Similarly with prayer, most people do not feel like praying when they start out, but they press in — 90 percent them, 10 percent God. As they keep going, it turns around and becomes 90 percent God and 10 percent them. The Spirit takes over as we yield to Him, yet we must come in faith.

Receiving the Spirit's power and refreshing is often the same way. It can be 90 percent you at first, standing there saying, "Well, I think maybe I feel something on me, but I could resist this." Yes, you can, but do not. Let Him come upon you. Let Him take you and fill you. Do not expect instant visions and dreams or other powerful manifestations that other people you may know about have had. You will have your own unique experience with God. Just let Him continue His work in you.

SOAK IN THE SPIRIT

Our ministry teams are trained to pray for everyone individually. That is why I don't just pray en masse saying,

"Come, Holy Spirit," and only see ten or fifteen percent of those present receive. We've learned to soak people in prayer, to keep praying for them, saying, "Give them more, Lord. Give them more."

Intimacy takes time, and so it is the same with God. We don't receive all God has for us with one quick touch. Our team prays for people while they're standing and continues to pray while they're shaking or laughing and even after they've fallen. People who fall usually start thinking about getting back up. But we encourage people not to get up quickly, but just to lie there and take another wave of the Spirit.

As our ministry teams continue to pray for people, they are led by the Spirit concerning what to pray for each person. They pray that what God wants in people will go in and what He wants out will come out. Pain, fear, hurt, depression, sin — even demons — may come out. Peace, joy, love, refreshing may come in. That is the kingdom of God — some things in, some things out. We are strengthened as a result.

We call this whole process of continuing prayer "soaking" someone. The person is getting soaked in prayer and in the Holy Spirit. This may go on for ten minutes or two hours. Soaking prayer seems to help people receive more and more of God. We want to marinate them in the Holy Spirit.

Some are surprised when I ask them not to pray in English (or whatever language) nor in tongues, while they are being "soaked" or prayed for. They wonder why. Prayer is a giving out ministry. It is hard to be pouring out while the Holy Spirit is pouring in. When people pray in tongues while we are praying for them, it is unlikely that they will receive more of God because when they are focused on giving, they are not receiving. It's difficult to pour out (pray) and let God pour in at the same time — just like it's hard to drink and talk. Receive first, then pray later.

96

A pastor from British Columbia learned this at one of our meetings in May 1994. John Overholt, pastor of Willow Point Foursquare Church in Campbell River, faxed me his experience. He came hungry and expecting, but found himself trying too hard to receive. One of our ministry teams' members encouraged him to relax and for the moment, stop praying in tongues. John relates:

> I then started to take note of all my resistance and striving. I also felt the presence of the Lord so strong you could cut it with a knife. I was determined that if I was going to be moved, it was going to be God who did so and not man. It didn't take long before my knees started to buckle and I was prostrate on my back with what seemed like waves of the Holy Spirit rolling over me, and yet I was very peaceful.
>
> Then the Lord started to show me some things about myself — my controlling nature, my competitiveness, my judgments toward other churches. So I repented of these things. I understand that the Holy Spirit is indeed a wonderful Counselor. After a few hours on the floor I started to fall more and more in love with the Lord and gained a greater passion to seek more of Him.

Often we need this preparation of soaking prayer to receive all God has for us. Jesus compared us to wineskins holding new wine.

> No one pours new wine into old wineskins. If he does, the new wine will burst the skins, the wine will run out and the wineskins will be ruined. No, new wine must be poured into new wineskins (Luke 5:37-38).

What is a wineskin? In ancient times, people took a goatskin and made a leather bag out of it. They worked and prepared the leather, then filled it with new wine. The wine, of course, was fermenting; therefore, it would stretch the bag. When the bag became empty, it would be flattened out and put aside.

What happens to a leather bag that is used to being moist and then is folded up and put it away somewhere? It becomes dry and stiff. The leather bag then needs to be renewed by soaking it in water — thoroughly immersing it. That is what the Holy Spirit is doing with some of us — just soaking us! That is why we believe in soaking prayer.

After the wineskin had been soaked, it softened again. They would inflate it, rub olive oil in it, and it would become resilient again. It was ready for the new wine.

We became new wineskins when we were born again. Maybe some of us were involved in the charismatic renewal twenty-five years ago. But just like the church at Ephesus that lost her first love, so had some of us. Our wineskins became stiff and dried out. Now God is renewing them.

I have watched many kinds of people. For some, at first, it seems as if there is no riverbed in their hearts; the anointing cannot flow. Others are so dry that the anointing seems to run off at first. But as they continue to "soak," the riverbed is cut into their hearts, and it opens more and more until there is a flow. When we soak people in prayer, it is almost as if their hearts open up more and more, and then more of God's presence and refreshing can flow in.

As we "soak" people in prayer, we often see two phases of God's moving in them. First, they are refreshed and healed and fall in love with Jesus again. This often then transitions into a phase of empowering for ministry.

The Holy Spirit brings in peace, joy, cleansing, transformation and healing. Then comes empowerment. They may speak in tongues. The empowering may be for prophecy, healing or evangelism. It is often accompanied by shaking as great power flows in and through them.

We have observed that with this new move of the Spirit, our capacity to receive from God is tremendously increased. Before, only a few would receive something deep in the Spirit. Now many receive a high-powered spiritual experience which causes *them* to ask *us* to explain what happened. They are surprised by the intensity of the Holy Spirit's power.

God wants us to continually be filled with the Spirit — and know that we are. He wants us to minister out of an overflow rather than with our spiritual tanks about empty. So we keep praying, "More, Lord." And He keeps giving more of His Spirit to us in an intimate way.

Why not pray for one another at home? Put on your favorite worship music and let your heart soak in the presence of the Lord. What a wonderful way to spend an hour or so with God. Allow Him to fill you again and again.

WHAT HAPPENED TO ME?

I continued to receive by faith whenever people prayed for me, yet God caught up to me one day, and I received a fresh touch of the Spirit! Carol and I went to Hamilton, Ontario, during the freezing cold January of 1994. We were invited for meetings with Pastor Bruce Woods at Hamilton Christian Fellowship. Renewal had only just broken out in our church. At the end of the meeting, one of their worship leaders came and gave me a prophetic word in perfect rhyme.

I remember wondering how this was possible — revealing the secrets of my heart and making it all rhyme poetically — and it was all happening so fast. I felt like a watermelon that had been cut right down the middle and laid open, exposed and vulnerable to Him.

"Oh God, You found me!" was my reaction. "God, You

found me. You came and You cut right into my heart."

I grabbed hold of a column I was standing beside, and I spiraled down to the ground. Some who were watching laughed and laughed, finding it hilariously funny. My heart was engaged with God, yet I was thinking, "If this is really God, how come I can still think? I am still aware of the room and everything that's going on."

My expectation was that I would be out if God came upon me powerfully and not aware of things around me. But most people are very aware of the room and the other people around. I certainly was, yet I went down because I could not stand up. The Holy Spirit came powerfully on me.

Later we went to the parking lot to go back to the motel. It was 1:00 A.M., and the laughter hit me right there in the parking lot. Our ministry team kept talking about it and cracking up in laughter. Whenever they mentioned it, that same laughter hit me again, and I laughed and laughed. My mind, however, was saying, "What are you laughing at? What is so funny? There is nothing funny at all." I didn't know, but I was falling apart with laughter.

Eventually we got in the car, started the motor, and it all hit me again. My mind did not understand what was going on. We went into McDonald's, and it hit me again, but by now it was becoming great fun. I was aware of God's presence and peace. It has happened a couple of times since then.

This presence and fellowship of the Holy Spirit is for everybody. He is a love gift from God the Father to you — and not just once, but day after day after day you can be continually filled with the Holy Spirit. My prayer is, "God, I must have more of You."

TRUST GOD WITH YOURSELF

In our meetings we have a ministry team who lays hands on people; the blessing is transferred and the people are filled with God. It is a "jump start" to get things going. It is wonderful and helpful.

Yet I believe your best and most meaningful times with the Lord will be alone in your prayer closet, praying to your Father in secret. The Father who sees in secret will reward you openly (Matt. 6:4).

Be vulnerable with God. Sometimes I tell people to leave the meeting and go back to their hotel rooms to be alone with God. Whatever it takes for you to open your heart up to Him, do it. Choose to walk toward Him in faith and say, "Lord, I am going to come to You. I am going to believe that You are the rewarder of those who diligently seek You, and I am going to ask You for bread. You won't give me a stone. You are going to give me the bread of heaven."

Understand that you can totally trust the Holy Spirit. I have often said, "Listen, if there is a person in all of the world that you can trust, then that person has to be the Holy Spirit." You can trust Him. You can go to Him and say, "Holy Spirit will You please come and fill me, touch me," and be perfectly safe in so doing.

Find that secret place of the Most High; abide under the shadow of the Almighty and start to love Him. Begin to know His heart. Get to know Him relationally, because it is not merely about an experience — it is about an intimate relationship with God. If you have this kind of a powerful and personal time with God, when you come down from the mountain top, people will receive the Spirit when you pray for them, too.

Having said all this, be aware that the Holy Spirit is a powerful reality. When Peter and John joined Philip for ministry in Samaria, the reality of the Spirit was so evident that a leading sorcerer wanted to buy the power (Acts 8:18-19). ✪

CHAPTER 7

FEARS: ROADBLOCKS TO RECEIVING

When we come to God with an open, surrendered, childlike heart and ask for the Holy Spirit, we will receive Him because we receive everything from God by faith. But sometimes things in our hearts block our ability to open up completely to God.

I discovered that the crux of my inability to receive more freely from God involved two basic issues: fear and pride. In this chapter I'll discuss the hindrance that fear is. Then in the next chapter I'll go into pride and how to get it out of your path in order to have intimacy with God.

Because we are afraid of certain things, people or situations, we put controls in place that safeguard us against becoming vulnerable or getting hurt again. Many of us contend with fears that control us and keep us from going ahead with God in faith.

Southern Baptist Pastor Gary Folds from Macon, Georgia, found out about fears and intimacy when he visited our church in December 1994 at the urging of some trusted friends (Jack Taylor and others). He admits he came "filled with apprehension, doubt and some fear."

Pastor Folds was somewhat overwhelmed during the first meeting — lots of praise music, people dancing all around the room, a few hundred people lying on the floor after prayer. He did not go up for prayer, but instead listened, walked around and watched curiously. He observed, "There were a few like myself who didn't know what to think of all this, but we were in a vast minority."

Pastor Folds admits that normally he would have been very critical about what he saw, but he felt the peace of God and the presence of the Holy Spirit very clearly.

> With each passing day I found myself drawn more and more into the presence of the Lord and a relationship with Him. I began to be a little jealous that everyone seemed to be having special encounters and I wasn't.
>
> Then it was as if the Holy Spirit spoke to my heart and confirmed that I might just be having the greatest manifestation of all. I was in the midst of what at one time would have caused me to turn tail and run, but now I was enjoying what I sensed to be the presence of God's power. My tendency to criticize was gone. I was not anxious, nor was I in a hurry. I was experiencing perfect peace in the midst of what at one time would have been storms

103

to me. With each passing day the time became more and more precious. I began to look forward to spending time in His presence in a way that I hadn't before. My, how good our God is.

How beautifully God allowed this pastor to press through his fears into intimacy.

GOD IS BIGGER THAN OUR FEARS

The Christian church, and particularly the charismatic movement, is in a major reaction to fear right now. Books and articles documenting every form of spiritual abuse and every wrong theological tangent have left us extremely "streetwise" and without childlike trust and faith. Elaborate documents claim that most of the church has been seduced, penetrated and corrupted by Satan through the New Age movement, Eastern mysticism and false doctrine. Some Christians seem to think Satan is stealing away Christ's church while the Holy Spirit just sits and watches.

Some of us have become afraid to trust in anything we are taught because someone somewhere has torn that teaching or experience apart. We want the truth, but we have lost our nerve to look for it.

Some years ago when I read some of those books, arguments and articles, I felt hopeless for several days saying, "What's the use? Why don't we quit? There is no way we can win. God doesn't care. Everybody is lost. We might as well do something else, make some money and hold up till the end, just trying to survive."

I had forgotten how big God really is. It took me three days to say, "Wait a minute, we have a big God. We have a great, big God!"

God is the One who holds the universe together. Think about how big the universe is. Our planetarium in Toronto had a map at one time with the galaxies, stars and planets. It was a huge chart that covered a whole wall. On it was a little sign that said, "You are here." Earth was a tiny speck on the chart, and it made me think, "Look at the size of the universe compared to earth."

Yet God, our Father, holds the whole thing in the palms of His hands. He holds it together by His powerful word (Heb. 1:3). Do you think He can take care of this tiny little planet? Do you think He can take care of His church? Can He take care of you and me? Yet we fret, "I wonder if God will see me through?" Many of us have a wonderful theology of the sovereignty of God, yet we can believe that Satan could steal God's church.

I love that song we used to sing which said, "He is big enough to rule the mighty universe, yet small enough to live within the heart."[1] God is so big — and yet small enough to be interested in the number of hairs on our heads (Matt. 10:30). Now, I really love my wife; I tell her every day, but I have never counted the number of hairs on her head. God has though.

We have a big God who tenderly cares for us. We don't need to fear. Fear will shut down our faith and cause us to withdraw and play it safe. Let's uncover these fears and discover how to move past them and receive all God has for us.

FEAR OF EMOTIONS

Who gave us our emotions? God did. Why? Because He is good. God has emotions, so we have them because we are made in His likeness. Obviously they are good.

Yet we have a fear of being emotional. We are cautioned, "Be careful. I hear they get real emotional over at those meetings. Watch out for emotionalism." Fear of being emotional may be causing some of us to avoid seeking after God wholeheartedly.

Do little children fear being too emotional? When was the

last time you saw a six-year-old who was afraid of being too emotional? Children don't worry about that. They simply laugh and cry and take life as it comes without denying who they really are. God told us to come to Him as little children. Some of us need to "get real."

> But the fruit of the Spirit is love, joy, peace, patience, kindness, goodness, faithfulness, gentleness and self-control. Against such things there is no law (Gal. 5:22).

What would love be like without the emotional component? It's almost impossible to imagine just a cold commitment. How about peace? Peace is a feeling of well-being. And where would our joy be contained if not in our feelings? These characteristics are not merely intellectual, psychological or only from the will. Kindness, gentleness and joy, each involves emotion.

When the Holy Spirit comes He brings these qualities into our lives. What kind of a person is the Holy Spirit? He is loving; He is joyful; He is peaceful; He is gentle; He is patient; He is kind; He is good; He is faithful; He is controlled. That is His personality.

You cannot get too much joy. You cannot get too much peace. We don't say, "Oh, you are over the limit; you have too much peace. You are sinning now." There is no law against these virtues. Maybe you are thinking, "What about self-control?" Well, the Holy Spirit brings us self-control to use against sin, not against the things of God.

Some have argued that people who laugh and shake, unable to stop, are "out of control"; therefore, they say, it cannot be from God. But the scripture in Galatians is referring to the fruit of the Holy Spirit in a person's life — the results of an encounter with God, not the encounter itself.

You cannot simply take a "snapshot" of people having powerful, religious experiences and then accuse them of being out of control. You must make a "movie" of their lives and in the aftermath, evaluate.

Do we reprimand Paul for having no self-control when he was knocked to the ground by God on the road to Damascus? (Acts 9). Was Peter out of control when he fell into a trance and had a vision from God? (Acts 10). Or was Zacharias, who could not talk for nine months? (Luke 1:20). We are not told what these experiences looked like, but it must have appeared strange, to say the least. If we are seemingly "out of control," it doesn't necessarily follow that we are out of God's control. What were the results in these men's lives? God was glorified. The fruit was of the Holy Spirit, and it was good.

James Clinkscales, financial minister of Lake Country Baptist Church in Ft. Worth, Texas, came to our church in March 1995 and attended four nights of services. In his hotel room, the Holy Spirit convicted him of his lifelong control of his emotions, especially toward those he loved. But he left disappointed that he had not had a more powerful encounter with God. James had decided by the last night that all the people on the floor were faking it, and he felt almost numb. He booked an early flight back on Sunday morning and left. He later wrote and told me:

> Somewhere at thirty-one thousand feet above St. Louis, I realized my unforgiveness toward my pastor of thirteen years and purposed to ask his forgiveness if I could get back to church before the morning service ended. Suddenly, the awesome presence of God's love and peace overwhelmed me as I sat on the aisle seat on the crowded airplane. My body vibrated with spiritual electricity for at least thirty minutes, and the Lord "rewired" my brain, soul and emotions. I wept openly and shook but didn't care who saw me. My Jesus

became so very, very real. As I listened to a worship tape on my Walkman, I lifted my hands in
praise. After the energy flow stopped, I tried to go
back to the rest room but could barely walk.

Mr. Clinkscales got to church by 11:30 A.M. and went to
the front to describe his plane ride and ask his pastor to
forgive him. Glory filled the church as most of the 150
people cried and applauded. He told me, "During the last
two weeks the church office, where I am the business man-
ager, has been filled with joy, praise and prayer."

This servant of God from Texas discovered that letting go
of his emotions to God brought healing and release.

The Holy Spirit wants to touch you deeply, influencing
and affecting your heart. If you fear releasing your emotions, then when you begin to experience the emotion of
love from the Holy Spirit you may shut right down.

Paul Reid, a pastor from Belfast, Ireland, wrote me about
an older lady who had been taught to stay away from emotional things all her life. Now that she is filled with the Spirit
and has a radical love affair going on with Jesus, her emotions have been set on fire. She is so in love with Him, but
she is upset saying, "Why didn't somebody tell me before
that all of this was available to the Christian? I have gone
through my entire life thinking that God was not in favor of
our having emotions like this, and I steered clear of everything that looked like it might be emotional or perhaps
even be fun." How tragic for her. Her fear of emotionalism
blocked the blessings for her.

We do not want to be led and controlled by emotionalism,
but neither do we want to take the emotional component
out of the Christian faith and be left with only a cerebral theology. Christianity is much more than that. It involves a full
range of emotional and relational interactions with God.

Pastor Brian Lucas and his wife from Christian Life Center

in Sydney, Australia, testified in one of our meetings. He knew little of his father because he had been listed "missing, presumed dead" in World War II when the British navy ship he was on went down. His family always hoped he might still be alive, even after the war. Pastor Lucas was a little boy when this happened, and whenever he heard footsteps on the street, he'd rush to the window, hoping it was his father returning.

After this pastor had been in several meetings in Australia in which he was touched by God, he was watching *Shadowlands,* a movie about C. S. Lewis, the famous author whose mother had died when he was a child. The person interviewing him wondered whether he ever expected to hear his mother's footsteps in the hallway. Upon hearing this, Pastor Lucas was reminded of his father, and he burst into uncontrollable sobs, crying for twenty minutes. He confesses:

> I realized that I had never grieved for my father because we never knew if he was dead. It just sort of petered out into nothingness, and he didn't come home. God really healed me that night of the grief that was tied up inside. He's released a lot of the emotion in me that I'd kept a really tight grip on in my life. He's taken the lid off that, and I've experienced some emotions that have been really hard to handle since then — but some have been really good.

I then asked his wife to confirm this. Family members are the ones who really notice changes. She admitted:

> I've noticed that he gets angry, and he never got angry before. He'd always kept it in, and he's having to learn how to handle that. It might sound really weird, but to be able to let that anger come

109

out and let the Lord deal with it has caused a tremendous change in him, and I praise God for it.

Now that's a new one, isn't it? This lady is happy because now her husband has learned to get angry. It's all part of being set free as a human being. Give yourself permission to let your emotions be expressed. Be real!

FEAR OF BEING DECEIVED

Nobody wants to be deceived, but neither do we want to overreact in fear, which we Christians sometimes do. "Did you pray through your house again today? Did you put oil on the bumpers of your car? Watch out that you don't get deceived. Watch out about this, watch out about that. Be careful."

I met a man some years ago who had a marker containing olive oil. Everywhere he went he made little crosses on everything. If he came into your house he marked everything from the door knob on. You may laugh, but I think that if the devil cannot stop you, sometimes he will push you too far. Many Christians have this fear of being deceived. When we take a biblical practice such as anointing or rubbing on of oil and push it to extremes with no fruit, we are apt to bring reproach on the Lord.

When you come to receive something from God, you can't ask in faith if you're half expecting a counterfeit. *We have to have more faith in God's ability to bless us than in Satan's ability to deceive us.* We have a great big God. The devil is very small in comparison to God!

> Which of you, if his son asks for bread, will give him a stone? (Matt. 7: 9).

> Which of you fathers, if your son asks for a fish, will give him a snake instead? Or if he asks for an

110

egg, will give him a scorpion? If you then, though you are evil, know how to give good gifts to your children, how much more will your Father in heaven give the Holy Spirit to those who ask him! (Luke 11:11-13).

If you ask for the Holy Spirit, you won't get a demon. If you fall down and shake and rattle and roll after you ask for the Holy Spirit, have you then received an unholy spirit? No. You received what you asked for according to Luke 11 — the Holy Spirit.

How do you know that you will not get a counterfeit? Well, tell me about your heart. Do you know that your heavenly Father loves you? "Well, I think so." Do you know what kind of a wonderful Father He is? "I think so." Well then, why would you think that if you asked Him for something good, He would allow Satan to give you a counterfeit? It's really so simple; it's simply a matter of trusting God. The manifestations are not the proof. The fruit in the heart is the proof! (Matt. 7:16).

Carl Buffington, rector of the Episcopal Church of the New Covenant in Winter Springs, Florida, wrote in his church newsletter after visiting us. He talked about seeing some flesh, some "acting out," but he continued:

> After being there, I have to say, the presence of God and His unconditional love dominate the atmosphere! It is the ambiance of the Holy Spirit. If the devil is behind it, as some say, he is doing himself in, because people are falling in love with their Lord and He is letting them know His love for them.

What spirit produces greater love for Jesus? Only the *Holy* Spirit. Remember what Jesus said after the teachers of the law accused Him of having a demon:

111

> If a kingdom is divided against itself, that kingdom cannot stand. If a house is divided against itself, that house cannot stand. And if Satan opposes himself and is divided, he cannot stand; his end has come (Mark 3:24-26).

If people think they could be drawn into a deceptive web and then out of nowhere Satan will come and let them have it saying, "Gotcha, sucker," then think they have given Satan too much ground. Instead, we are to believe the scripture that says we are in the Father's hands and no one can pluck us out (John 10:29).

P. J. Hanley, a former skeptic from New York, said of this renewal:

> If it is of the devil, then the devil has had a conversion experience. Since when has he been in the business of increasing love for God and exalting the King of kings? Since when has he been the source of peace, joy and righteousness? I have no further doubt in my mind that this is the beginning of a significant move of the Holy Spirit which we have all been waiting for. My advice to those of you who are skeptical or troubled by it all is to examine the fruit. Taste and see for yourself.

If we do not know God's heart and His ways, and if we do not trust Him, we may think something we do not understand is from the devil, and we will quench it. It is not wrong to quench things, but it is wrong to quench the works of the Holy Spirit.

It is amazing how the fear of deception will short-circuit the faith of many who desperately need a fresh touch from heaven. Attributing the works of the Holy Spirit to Satan is a very serious offense. If there is even a small chance that something may be of God after all, we would do well to consider the pharisee Gamaliel's counsel to the Sanhedrin when they brought Peter and the apostles before them.

> Leave these men alone! Let them go! For if their purpose or activity is of human origin, it will fail. But if it is from God, you will not be able to stop these men; you will only find yourselves fighting against God (Acts 5:38-39).

God loves us. He is faithful, and He will not give something false to us. We have to come to Him in faith. We are not coming expecting a counterfeit. We are not coming expecting to get deceived. We are coming to God and expecting to receive more of the Holy Spirit!

> Without faith it is impossible to please God, because anyone who comes to him must believe that he exists and that he rewards those who earnestly seek Him (Heb. 11:6).

FEAR OF PHENOMENA AND MANIPULATION

Some of us are afraid that the unusual phenomena we've heard about might happen to us!

A Lutheran pastor came to a pastors' meeting in early 1994 and said to Carol, "I am so afraid of falling. Would you mind if I just lie down on the floor?" She was surprised but said, "No, go ahead." The man lay down on the floor. Then she prayed for him, and the Spirit of God came upon him powerfully. He got the whole issue of falling out of the way. Consider the effect simply lying down had on this pastor.

When my wife first told me about this incident, I felt something was not real with it. But as I reconsidered, I had to admit that nothing in Scripture would prohibit lying down to receive prayer. This pastor's motives were obviously right, and God came to him wonderfully. He had

113

simply dealt with his fear in an acceptable, childlike way.

Some people are afraid of the phenomena because they don't want to be vulnerable. Have you noticed that you are out of your comfort zone when you are lying on the floor or when you are shaking? You feel like everybody is watching you. You feel vulnerable. You think that somebody could step on you or that you look foolish.

Faith, vulnerability and humility are necessary ingredients to receive more from God. We need to say, "Lord, whatever You want to do, I am open to it. I want more of You."

Carl Kinbar, a pastor from Kingston, New York, pressed through his anxiety about manifestations and met God. He wrote me that he was the one who had rebuked me for not preaching repentance in a meeting he attended. He added:

> What I didn't tell you, and couldn't admit to myself at the time, was that I was in great conflict over what I had seen that evening. I had come to those meetings specifically to confirm to myself and our church that this "laughing thing" was definitely not from God. And yet I couldn't deny that what I had seen was real and supernatural.

That night Pastor Kinbar prayed and read through a book about past revivals. He became convinced that this was from God. He had never imagined what it was like in the midst of one of those meetings with all the manifestations and such. When he came to a pastor's meeting the next afternoon, he had an intense hunger to be touched by God. He was not disappointed. He spent two and a half hours on the floor with the Holy Spirit convicting him deeply of his need for more of Him.

> He showed me that I was deeply wounding my teenage son with my words (I wept for perhaps half an hour). He led me into gut-wrenching

114

intercession for my friend's backslidden son, and then filled me with the most incredible peace and joy that I've ever known. This visitation has changed my relationship with my God and with my son.

Pastor Kinbar stumbled at the manifestations until God broke through. Maybe for you it's not manifestations but manipulation you fear. In the past you may have encountered an evangelist or pastor who did not think he looked good if you did not fall over, so he wanted to help you fall. Some evangelists have just developed a forceful style, and I suppose that is OK. But when that has happened to me, I have felt manipulated.

If I was standing there expecting something from God and somebody pushed me hard or subtly kept increasing the pressure on my head until I fell over, my mind became focused on my own balance. Then my focus was on me. Where should it have been? Yes, on Jesus.

This manipulation can make people afraid of experiencing any manifestations from God. Yet there are times when the Holy Spirit comes upon people so strongly they feel like they were pushed, even though they weren't. If that happens here in our meetings and the person thinks we pushed him, I say, "Let's do it again and I will pray from three feet back." Then he knows it was God who touched him.

A pastor from Arizona came to Toronto grudgingly, led by God just "to look." He had been prayed for and pushed backward before in his life, and he was "repelled" by that. But he promised the Lord he would stay the week in Toronto regardless of what happened.

He went to the back of the church for prayer as instructed and waited for someone to pray for him. He tells what happened next:

Something, someone had jerked me off my feet, and I landed on my back and my feet went

115

straight up in the air. God showed me that He's doing whatever's happening here. It doesn't take someone coming by, necessarily, and placing a hand on you or even getting near you. The proximity of a human is not necessary. My attitude changed quickly.

This pastor cried as he told our church that he had been pastoring for thirty years and had come to the point that he hated ministry. He quit three years ago. "I didn't like people," he confessed. Everyone laughed gently with him as he added, "and that's bad for a pastor." Through his sobs he told us that through the prayer here, he's already beginning to like people again.

From our perspective, we don't care if you fall and manifest something or not. What is really important is that you have a meaningful touch from God that deeply impacts your heart.

Press in to Jesus and confess your fear of the phenomena or of being manipulated. Let Him release you from that, and then receive on His terms.

FEAR OF BEING HURT AGAIN

Hurts and fears in our lives have taught us not to trust. When I suggest to some people that they open up to God, they think, "No way! I'm not going to be vulnerable to anyone again."

People who have been abused in some way have an even more difficult time trusting God with control of their lives. Many have been abused physically, emotionally or sexually. Often there is a nagging fear controlling them, and they feel if they ever let things get out of hand they are going to get hurt again. They have become very streetwise and suspicious, and that is the opposite of childlike faith.

If this has happened to you, get help to work through the

fears and the feelings toward the people who abused you. Then you can forgive. Forgiveness is the only way out of this prison. Get untangled so you can come in simplicity to the Lord. Learn to trust Him so you are not always wary, "What is the catch here? Why do they want me to fall over? What do they want from me?"

Everything we receive from the Lord works by faith. What does that mean? It means we have to trust Him. We have to put our hand in His hand and say, "Father, I really trust You. I trust You with my life. I will let the Holy Spirit take charge. I will give You control."

As I said before, if there's anyone you can trust in the whole world, it's the Holy Spirit. Surrendering to God will be the best thing that ever happened to you. Give God control. He wants to heal your hurts, not hurt you more.

FEAR CAUSED BY WRONG THEOLOGY

Many of us have been taught against manifestations of the Holy Spirit — speaking in tongues and so on. We have heard that Satan can show up in power, but the Holy Spirit can't or doesn't. Everything has been called into question.

When leaders who do not understand what God is doing write and speak against it, they can create the fear of deception in the hearts of people. Then people will not press into God, instead they back away from what they think is extreme and fanatical. This fear can crush revival — in hearts and in cities. It happened in Lystra a long time ago.

Paul and Barnabas went into Lystra and, among other things, healed a man who was born lame. The people were recognizing the wonderful fruit that resulted from the manifest presence and anointing of God. They attributed the fruit to Paul and Barnabas though and were going to make sacrifice to them, thinking they were gods. However, Paul and Barnabas prevented that, but there was still great joy in the city.

The very next day some religious leaders showed up — people with no power, no anointing, no good news, only arguments. They won the crowd over, causing the people to draw back, fearing that what they had experienced was a counterfeit. That fear drove the crowd to act.

> They stoned Paul and dragged him outside the city, thinking he was dead. But after the disciples had gathered around him, he got up and went back into the city. The next day he and Barnabas left for Derbe (Acts 14:19-20).

So Paul and Barnabas left town. That is the real tragedy! Lystra missed a great move of God that came to them. Revival missed that city. What might have happened if the people had not been talked out of believing what they had seen with their own eyes?

The same thing happened when Jesus went to His home town, Nazareth. The townspeople were going to throw Him off the cliff because they did not believe that He could be the Messiah (Luke 4). Revival in the hearts of those home-town folks might have come if Jesus had been welcomed there.

Allowing wrong teaching and wrong theology to paralyze you and bring fear into your heart can stop your own personal revival. Instead, be like children, pressing into God with simple faith, asking your heavenly Father for bread. For further study on this, obtain the teaching tape from Jack Taylor entitled "Confessions of a Pharisee."[2] It is an excellent word.

FREEDOM FROM FEARS

I encourage you to come to God with absolutely no agenda. If you have been manipulated before, forgive the person. Ask God to heal your heart on these issues and let them go. If you are afraid of shaking, laughing or falling on the floor, talk to God about it. Explore the reasons you fear these manifestations. Then ask yourself, "If God is really doing this, am I willing to let Him do this with me?"

When we get fearful, we stop taking risks and start trying to tidy up everything that might offend. We take control. Ask God to forgive you for submitting to controlling fears, even unconsciously. Repent and choose vulnerability. Tell God, "I will risk being vulnerable with You. I'm choosing to trust You."

As long as you set the parameters and decide what you will give into and what you will not give into, you are limiting what He can and cannot do in you. Go with intimacy and let Him come and touch you profoundly and fill you and fill you and fill you. You can analyze it and test it later.❂

CHAPTER 8

PRIDE: HINDRANCE TO INTIMACY

There is something within all of us that likes to boast about our superior knowledge, position or abilities. It's called pride. Pride is very destructive to an intimate relationship with God. It keeps us in control instead of God. It prevents total surrender to Him.

Pride causes us to avoid doing things that are beneath our dignity or can cause us embarrassment or losing favor with our peers. It cries out for justice when we are hurt by others: "I deserve better than this."

But we are called to humility, to take the lowly seat, to be the servant of all. If we hold onto our pride, we exclude close relationship with God because the scripture says, "God opposes the proud but gives grace to the humble" (James 4:6).

In my case, I wanted to stay in control. I wanted to analyze what was happening. But my understanding and approval of what He is doing are not God's requirements for intimacy with Him. Intimacy will always require us to surrender our controlling pride in order to unite with Him in simple trust.

A pastor from Seattle, Washington, who visited our church in fall 1994 told me that he had always been conservative and professional. However, in a Sunday morning service he experienced "rolls of glory and laughter" while he was on the floor.

This pastor told me God restored him, "a pastor on the way out." But he was willing to be humbled, to have his pride broken, to receive from God.

Let's examine the different ways pride can invade our lives.

PRIDE OF BEING "COOL"

Our culture puts a very high value on being "cool." What does being cool mean? It means not reacting emotionally to things and appearing to be in control. Being "cool" means conforming your life, not to what you want, but to what your peer group thinks you should be like.

But this is a denial of our basic makeup. We were designed by God to express love, joy, peace, sorrow or anger. This crippling fear of not being "cool" will shut us down emotionally.

Years ago, Carol and I attended a church where they sang, "If you want joy you must sing for it; you must shout for it; you must jump for it." I used to hate that song, but Carol really got into it. As they sang, "you must jump for it," she jumped way up in the air, as high as she could jump — and I stood there watching her.

One day I said to her, half teasing but half serious too, "Honey, do you know what? It is really not cool to jump." She was shocked. She was in the presence of the Lord, and I had just poured a bucket of ice water over her. But she responded, "What? Well, I don't care. I want joy!"

You know, that smote my heart as if a sword went into me all the way to the hilt. I responded, "But wait a minute! I want joy, too." She looked at me with one eyebrow up and said, "Well...jump then. Get free. You're too concerned about what others might think."

This desire to remain emotionally flatlined is a major barrier to receiving the Holy Spirit because He will not play your game. This belief is called stoicism; it came from the Greeks. They denied their emotions in an attempt to become free from passion so they would not be moved by either joy or tragedy. That way they were protected against deep sorrow when all of the sorrows of life came. The Greeks believed that life was basically a tragedy.

This belief that being without emotions is "cool" has infiltrated deeply into Western culture and thinking. Many believe (especially men) that to show emotions is to show weakness.

I think Jesus thought it was cool to enter into the Father's presence, do the Father's will and worship the Father in Spirit and in truth. Let's be true to ourselves and to Jesus and not worry about being cool in other people's eyes. Let's call it what it really is — pride.

PRIDE OF THE MIND

You'll never find the heart of God with the mind; you find Him with the heart. It took me years to figure that out.

The mind of man is a marvelous tool. And the theology

we go by is vitally important. But it's used as a check and balance to make sure we're still on track. Our minds should not take the place of God; we should not throw away everything we can't figure out.

We have this notion that we need to understand everything God does before we "buy into it." Why do we base truth on our observations and understanding of things? Paul told the Corinthians:

> My message and my preaching were not with wise and persuasive words, but with a demonstration of the Spirit's power, so that your faith might not rest on men's wisdom, but on God's power (1 Cor. 2:4-5).

First, we see the power of God; then we receive the wisdom of God. That's the correct order. First you get impacted by God, then you ask, "What happened to me?" That's when you can get wisdom and understanding about what happened.

Can we dare think that something is not right and that it cannot be God unless we understand it? What kind of arrogant pride is that? Rather, we must have faith in God and what He does even when we do not always understand.

> "For my thoughts are not your thoughts, neither are your ways my ways," declares the Lord.
> "As the heavens are higher than the earth, so are my ways higher than your ways and my thoughts than your thoughts" (Is. 55:8-9).

A delightful woman came to Toronto from Europe. She came from an extremely theological and intellectual background — "too much thinking," she said. While under God's power she had a vision. Much to her surprise, Jesus took her through events of her childhood, and they relived them together.

This woman used to play soccer, and Jesus told her gently that she took the glory for herself. So she wept and repented, then they played soccer together. She laughed and laughed at His long robe, then she asked Him to be the goalkeeper. He was so strong, He knocked all the balls away. But then He let her have a goal, and she laughed some more.

Then Jesus told her she always acted like a boy. She said this was true because her father wanted a boy, and it hurt her. But Jesus showed her that He wanted her to be a girl. She explains that she saw, like a movie before her eyes, the yard she used to play in as a child. She had a pretty flowered dress on, and they danced together, and her hair blew in the wind. Jesus told her, "You know, forever — I wanted you as a girl." And she cried and cried. "It was so wonderful because He planned me to be a girl. It was so beautiful."

Another evening Jesus showed her herself as a baby, and He tickled her. She laughed and laughed, and baby noises came out of her. Another time, she was one year old. She was holding a toy, but she couldn't play with it because she didn't know how. And she looked into the eyes of Jesus and asked Him to explain how to play with this toy. And He took time and told her. She concluded, crying:

> From all of my background, I'm thinking, "Playing with Jesus — that's the *worst*." But that's so wonderful and so healing. I'm so glad. I know that I am not the same now. I have a brand new relationship with Jesus. He's so good; I didn't know that.

Jesus led this woman through an experience that offends the intellectual. It's hard to understand — playing with Jesus. But it was God. Let us agree here and now that we are not going to understand everything that God is doing for a long, long time.

This sort of experience sounds a lot like Joel 2, doesn't it? Dreaming dreams and seeing visions as the Holy Spirit is being poured out (v. 28).

When God is moving on you, your rational mind will often feel left out. The Holy Spirit is saying, "That's right. You yield control because this is a heart issue, and I am in control." That is the surrender part.

PRIDE OF ANALYZING AND STAYING IN CONTROL

That whole rational reasoning process can block you from intimacy and from receiving the Spirit's power. In my case it did because I was always analyzing.

Carol has often prayed for me, and I would stand there trying to receive from God, yet not feeling anything. I would say, "Honey, is the Holy Spirit flowing in?"

She would say, "Yes, just receive." Then she would say, "Whoops, where did you go?"

"What do you mean?"

"Well, you went somewhere, and God's anointing for you came back on me."

Some of you who minister know what that feels like. When you are praying for someone else and they do not receive, the anointing comes back to you and you just about fall over — either you or the person who is helping you.

I asked Carol why I didn't receive, and she told me that I was trying to stay in control. I argued with her, but she was more convincing: "You will not surrender; you will not give yourself to God."

I was trying to surrender with everything that was within me, but I became aware that often my mind was on things other than loving the Lord.

I realized that I was continuously monitoring my balance.

125

Since I have been pushed before, I was saying to myself, "I am not going anywhere unless this is really God." I would think, "I feel like I'm waving a little bit. Why? Is it because I have been standing so long? Or is God actually touching me?" I was unconsciously taking control and analyzing the entire process.

The Lord asked me one day, "When you go somewhere with three or four friends, who drives?" I responded, "Well, usually I would drive."

"Why?" He pressed.

"I guess I have learned that things go better when I drive."

Can you see how subtle this desire to control is? Do you prefer to drive when you are going somewhere with others? Perhaps for you, it's not driving — it's eating. You want to be in control of what's for dinner or which restaurant you go to. Or maybe it's free time — you want to decide what to do with it, not let others — or God — decide.

I became self-reliant at an early age. My father was seldom around. Oh, he loved me — he told me so many times. I loved him, too, but he was just never there. He would make promises that he would not keep. And I learned in my heart of hearts that if I wanted something done, I had to do it myself.

The lesson is not all bad, but it didn't lead me into a trusting dependency on my heavenly Father who does deliver on His promises and who is really there for me.

You might ask, "What if God makes me do something foolish? What if I get embarrassed? What if I let go of control and God requires difficult things of me?"

Well, we have to know the character of God, don't we? We have to know that He is trustworthy, that He wants the best for us. You see, God wants to "drive." Isn't that strange? He wants to be God. He wants to be in control, and we have to hand over the wheel, give Him the right to decide what we are going to do. This is where faith and trust come in.

An Anglican vicar, Reverend Mike Houston from Buckinghamshire, England, came to our services in February 1995. He had no previous experiences with any manifestations of the Holy Spirit and only agreed to come out of general interest and to support members of his congregation who were interested in this "real and exciting stuff."

After the first night meeting, he felt that what he saw was of God, but it was not for him. In fact, he was pleased that he had survived without succumbing. At the next morning service during worship, he began to feel the presence of the Holy Spirit. He explained:

> We were all on our knees in prayer, singing "Mercy is falling like sweet spring rain," when feelings of such joy and peace overwhelmed me that I had no choice but to slip elegantly sideways amongst seats and feet, onto the carpet. It was unexpected but a truly wonderful, humbling experience. I knew at once that I was loved and affirmed. I no longer doubt.

Though this vicar struggled to maintain control and not "succumb" to God, when he did let go he discovered that God loved him. All doubt fled. God is indeed trustworthy; His character is good.

The best thing we can do with our minds when we're receiving from God is to focus on Jesus. Worship helps you receive and enter into intimacy. Do not take control, do not resist, do not analyze; just surrender to His love. You can analyze the experience later; just let it happen.

PRIDE OF SETTING THE TERMS WITH GOD

Thousands of years ago Naaman was a commander in the army of Aram (Syria), a pagan nation. He had leprosy. His wife's maid was an Israeli girl who had been taken captive. She told Naaman's wife about Elisha the prophet, saying that he could heal Naaman.

So Naaman set out to find Elisha, bringing with him gold, silver and clothing, thinking that these gifts might help him get healed. He came to the prophet of God and knocked on the door. But Elisha did not meet with Naaman; instead he sent out his servant with the unusual instructions for Naaman to take a bath in the Jordan seven times in order to be healed.

> But Naaman went away angry and said, "I thought that he would surely come out to me and stand and call on the name of the Lord his God, wave his hand over the spot and cure me of my leprosy. Are not Abana and Pharpar, the rivers of Damascus, better than any of the waters of Israel? Couldn't I wash in them and be cleansed?" So he turned and went off in a rage (2 Kin. 5:11-12).

Naaman was insulted that Elisha did not even have the courtesy to answer the door himself. Elisha didn't make any religious motions over him, and he had the nerve to tell him to go take a bath in the muddy Jordan for his cleansing and healing.

But Naaman wanted to set the terms. What Elisha had told him didn't make sense. Why the Jordan? Why not the rivers near his home in Damascus? Yet this was the Word of the Lord for Naaman. These were God's terms, and Naaman's healing would depend on meeting these conditions.

People often tell me they almost missed the Father's blessing by not coming to Toronto. They felt God had spoken to them to go to Toronto and be blessed, but they reasoned, "God, if You want to bless me, You can do it right here at home." Well, theologically, that is true. But if God says, "Go," then you'd better go. We must be humbly obedient and not let pride steal our blessings. Isn't it amazing how we want God to meet us on *our* terms?

Naaman went off in a rage, but thank God for Naaman's servants. These men must have been humble because they recognized the value of what was going on here. They diplomatically said to Naaman:

> If the prophet had told you to do some great thing, would you not have done it? How much more, then, when he tells you, "Wash and be cleansed"! (v. 13).

Naaman probably expected to be told something like, "Go to Mount Sinai, walk around it seven times, climb to the top, sacrifice seven bulls, come back here, give me all your money — walk — do not ride home, then you will be healed of your leprosy."

Hard tasks would have made sense to Naaman. They would have been reasonable "payment" for this miracle. They would have satisfied his pride. But God set His terms — the act God requested would demand humility and vulnerability.

So Naaman went to the Jordan and dipped himself once, twice. What was going through his mind, do you think? "OK, I will bathe three times, but I am not going to do this seven times." After the fourth time with no change, maybe he thought, "This is ridiculous. I am making a fool of myself."

Naaman is being humbled, isn't he? Maybe he was almost naked before all his servants and attendants. That means he revealed to them the extent of his leprosy. I can hear his servants saying, "Wow, his leprosy is much worse than I thought." Would they respect him again now that they knew?

We don't know how advanced his leprosy was, but it was certainly a serious problem for Naaman. We do get a clue, though, when Gehazi later inherits Naaman's leprosy and becomes "white as snow" (v. 27). What is obvious is that Naaman is being humbled and made vulnerable by this experience.

The seventh time he dipped, his flesh became like the flesh of a little child. All he had to do was go and dip in the Jordan seven times, and he was healed.

You see, if we want more from God, we have to let God set the terms. Maybe God's terms are going to the front of the church, having somebody pray for you, falling down on the carpet and lying there for a while. But some of us sit back and say, "I am not doing that. That's dumb, and I don't want to do it. I want You to bless me, Lord, while I am sitting right here in my chair. Lord, You come to me on my terms."

You may feel stupid lying on the floor in front of a whole lot of people, especially on a dirty floor. The devil is saying, "What a fool you are making of yourself." That's exactly what he was saying to Naaman as he got into the water. But Naaman wanted healing so bad that he persisted through the humbling, through being exposed as he really was. When our desire for more of God supersedes our pride, we become willing to come on God's terms.

Sometimes I say to my wife incredulously, "Every night now we preach, we pray for people, and they fall down on the carpet. Every night of our lives, this is what we do." Isn't that the craziest thing you ever heard?

But what is so amazing is that when people get up off the carpet, their "leprosy" is gone, and their hearts are transformed.

An Australian Christian school principal and his wife

came to our services in early 1995. This woman had been suffering with chronic fatigue syndrome for years. Plus, she had gone from enjoying the presence of God and being interested in her family to being emotionless, with no sense of God's presence. This principal wrote me, "We came here desperate, but believing God would meet us."

God worked with both husband and wife, bringing healing to each. This husband said:

> God was systematically tearing me apart. The time for me was one of tears and repentance. I had to repent of ten years of doing full-time ministry my way. Moreover, the Holy Spirit showed me how insensitive I was to Him and how often I quenched Him. More tears and repentance.

This newly humbled husband shared with his wife what God showed him — that he quenched the Holy Spirit — and she said, "That's what you do to me. I wonder if God will now give me that emotional release."

During the week they were here, they visited Niagara Falls. As they viewed the falls, this wife cried out, "It's happening. I feel so free and light inside. I know God has released me emotionally." Then she pointed out that Niagara Falls is often referred to as "the honeymoon capital of the world." They had never had a honeymoon. Her husbands writes, "God had met us and confirmed His love for us. He was honeymooning with us. We have been transformed and will never be the same again."

This husband was willing to be humbled, to quit doing things his way and let God set the terms. Therefore God broke through into their lives. You see, the things of God are beautifully simple, wonderfully childlike. We need to focus on Jesus, be children and enter in.

INTIMACY WITH GOD

During one season in my life years ago, I would become aware of God's presence close to me when I was praying. When I felt this I would quickly get out my "needs list."

"Lord," I would say, "we need a newer car, a bigger building, money for the church." But I noticed that His presence would draw back. I wondered why.

Years later, while reading in Exodus, I related to the deep and searching prayer of Moses, "Show me your glory" (33:18). I immediately cried out, "O Lord, why are You so hard to find? Why is it so difficult to be close to You?" I was thinking in terms of His holiness and my unholiness.

But He spoke to me in my heart, and His answer was one of the most precious things I ever heard God say to me: "When I reveal My heart to someone, I become very vulnerable."

I had never thought of God as being vulnerable. I thought of Him as omniscient, omnipotent and omnipresent, which, of course, He is. But He was sharing with me His own desire for fellowship, relationship and intimacy — and I was surprised. That's the nature of love — it needs to be freely and willingly reciprocated. He drew near to have fellowship and intimacy with me, and I was deeply hurting Him by immediately asking for things.

Then He spoke again saying, "Many of My people have married Me for My money." That devastated me. I wept and wept. I repented for inappropriately asking Him to bless my programs and agenda. "Lord, I'm so sorry! I don't just want Your stuff! I want You! I want intimacy and relationship with You. I want to be a son, well pleasing unto You."

Through this experience I realized that intimacy is based on humility, vulnerability and trust. We are often oblivious to the fact that God wants an intimate relationship with us. Intimacy cannot be a one-sided love affair. It flows out of humble, vulnerable hearts.

FREEDOM FROM PRIDE

Being free from the control of pride is not merely to be willing to fall on the floor or shake. The purpose is to be released to have the intimacy that accompanies those and any other experiences the Lord wants to take you through.

Repent of pride and choose to move into intimacy. Can you forget what people think? Can you expose yourself to God? Are you willing? He is trustworthy. He may humble you, but He will raise you up changed.

God, of course, can meet you anywhere. One of the best places is right at home, or wherever you are right now. Shut yourself in with God. Put some worship music on, and ride the worship right into heaven. Take half an hour or an hour and seek God. Enter into His presence and give Him your heart. Just enjoy God. Let Him bless and fill your life. Then you can analyze it — later. ❂

CHAPTER 9

THE PHENOMENA: QUESTIONS AND ANSWERS

D o they offend you and me?" I was thinking about all the phenomena we have seen in our meetings — everything from severe shaking to graceful dancing to being out cold for hours — and my reaction to it.

Then I remembered the time when Jesus asked His disciples that same question. He had just told them they needed to eat His flesh and drink His blood in order to enter His kingdom (John 6). Can you imagine what the disciples thought? "Has He gone mad? How can we follow a man who says things like this? That's outrageous! People will think we agree with these kind of crazy statements." Jesus knew what they were thinking. He asked:

Does this offend you? What if you see the Son of Man ascend to where he was before! (vv. 61-62).

Many of Jesus' disciples quit following Him after that. He let them leave. Perhaps He knew that what lay ahead would be more than they could take if they were offended at this.

I returned in my mind to my original question: "Do these manifestations offend me?" They certainly took all of us by surprise. This wasn't the quiet and reverent move of God we'd expected when we started praying for revival. Yet again and again, we have been astounded at the accounts of transformation in the hearts and lives of people which occur in the midst of all these manifestations.

"No," I decided. "They do not offend me." I love the manifestations because I know they're from God, and He's doing a great work in people when they occur. I want God's people to be free to respond to Him.

WHAT CAUSES THESE PHENOMENA?

We use the terms *phenomena* and *manifestations* to describe the unexplained things that happen to people physically during a powerful encounter with God. We may wonder if the Holy Spirit is actually causing what we see or if the phenomena are humans reaction to God's powerful presence. I believe it can be both.

Often when people fall down it is not because they are knocked down by the Holy Spirit, but rather their own human strength was overcome by the Spirit's overwhelming presence. Sometimes, even the powerful shaking is not because the Holy Spirit is deliberately shaking them, but rather they are reacting to His power and presence.

On the other hand, the Spirit can directly cause certain manifestations within people, such as striking the apostle Paul blind for three days. Manifestations of the Spirit like the gifts referred to in 1 Corinthians 12 are the deliberate intention of the Spirit, as seen in Acts 2:4 when the apostles spoke in tongues and prophesied according to Joel's prophecy (Joel 2:28).

Precisely what is taking place within a person is often difficult to discern. I believe it's possible for the Holy Spirit to come powerfully on a person and for demons to react to the Spirit's presence and be driven off. The flesh may respond inappropriately while a wonderful, sovereign and even prophetic work is being done in the person.

The gift of distinguishing of spirits should be something we continually pray for so we can discern the demonic from the human from the Holy. The astonishing thing is that again and again, as we trust God and allow Him to work within us, the end result is wonderful Christian fruit.

Keeping our eyes on the manifestations themselves is not the correct response. The manifestations are only the outward part of the Holy Spirit's work — the inner work is what's important.

Our God is powerful; He knows how to transform a heart, heal a body, cleanse from sin and release from fears. Current Christian thought may not allow for a God who works through noise and laughter and falling under His power. We must look at the God of the Bible — our God — not necessarily the God of twentieth century Christian thought. And our God does do these kinds of things.

THE FLESH AND THE DEMONIC

As I already pointed out, discernment is very important. Church leaders are particularly responsible if they allow the flesh and demonic activity to go on. A weighty accountability is on us to know what is from God and what is not. If we do not stop wrong manifestations, people can possibly be led into deception. But on the other hand, if we quench the Holy Spirit, we are in bigger trouble. There is a real call for care here.

Most people would agree that the phenomena we see have only three possible origins. They are either demonic, the flesh or the Holy Spirit. Our experience has been that manifestations of the flesh and the demonic are actually rare, though they tend to get all the attention. By far the majority of the manifestations in our meetings are the results of the Holy Spirit interacting with a person — body, soul and spirit. We need to create an atmosphere that welcomes the Holy Spirit and allows Him to do whatever work He wants to do.

But here is the challenge: That which is demonic must be dealt with — hopefully the person can be delivered from demonic influence. That which is the flesh must be pastored through correctly and redirected. That which is of the Holy Spirit must be embraced. Sometimes the manifestations look almost the same. Two people can be on the floor doing exactly the same thing, but one is under the anointing and the other person is wishing he was under the anointing. So, we need the Lord's wisdom, don't we?

If someone fakes it, saying in his heart, "I am going to fall down so that others will think I am receiving and that I am just as spiritual as anybody else," is that wrong? Yes. That is religious pride and a denial of reality.

Someone else may come for prayer then deliberately fall down just because he truly wanted God so desperately. His method may be wrong because he is trying to make it happen, but in his heart he really wants God. Is that so wrong?

When hurting people, as many of us are, get together and seek God, even if we do our best, everything won't be perfect. The flesh is nothing to fear but just something to deal with in the Lord's wisdom. Let's not throw the baby out with the bath water.

A pastor told us that as he was walking back to the hotel after attending a service here, he prayed, "God, surely You don't like fleshly manifestations. Why don't You do something about it?" The Lord gently spoke into his heart: "When you get to the point where you have no flesh for Me to judge, then I'll set you free to judge theirs."

The point is, every church has flesh to deal with. People fall asleep during meetings. They refuse to give financially to God's work. They criticize and find fault with one another. These are all manifestations of the flesh.

The fleshly manifestations associated with phenomena are often much easier to correct than these other areas I've mentioned. We often tell a person, in love, not to do a certain thing, and by and large, they respond positively. But correcting the fleshly manifestations of not giving to God's work or criticizing each other — that's much more difficult.

Sometimes we have asked people to stop a manifestation when we feel it is in the flesh. But even when someone is in the flesh, it is rarely 100 percent in the flesh. God is moving in them in some way, and they are learning how to deal with that. We try to err on the side of grace and help people learn and receive from God. Remember, He rewards those who seek Him diligently (Heb. 11:6); they will find Him. That's a promise from God.

A missionary to Russia commented after attending a Catch the Fire conference here: "I appreciate the tender pastoral atmosphere at the conference. We felt protected and cared for in a merciful way — for example, those who were on occasion out of the Spirit didn't get a ton of bricks on their heads."

Very rarely do we see a strong demonic manifestation. If this happens, we immediately command the demon to be quiet. We then urge the person to refocus on Jesus, to start again and receive more of the Holy Spirit. If the commotion continues, we take the person out of the service and work with him or her separately. We do not allow demonic manifestations to disturb the services or grab the focus and attention, but as I said, they are very rare.

I asked a group of pastors who were visiting our church what was the worst thing that could happen in a service like ours. They answered that the demons would display themselves instead of God. Then I asked them, "Well, if this is happening, I have one further question, are they coming in or going out?"

You see, if they're leaving, that's what we want, isn't it? That's what the Holy Spirit wants. In fact, we pray that what needs to go out will go out and what God wants to come in will come into people. It's simpler than we sometimes realize.

Pastor John Overholt, whom I mentioned before, wrote that a great release is happening in their church, Willow Point Foursquare Church in Campbell River, British Columbia. He points out, "Our people are being set free from long-standing bondages. We've had some major deliverances. It seems that when the Holy Spirit starts moving on people, any deep-seated demonic captivity is exposed and then flushed out."

How do we know if a manifestation is demonic or not? That's where the gift of discernment comes in, but it's usually not difficult. When people are being moved on by the Holy Spirit, we can still talk to them. We ask, "How are you? What's going on?" They are free to respond, telling us what is happening inside, how the Lord is moving on them.

But demons will be hostile to questions and prayer. They will be threatening to those praying for the person. They manifest strongly, sometimes with an attack against the ministry team. So it's not usually difficult to tell the difference.

It is helpful to know that God is taking some things out

of people and putting some things in. But He is the one who is doing it. He is in control. Somebody might scream and it's demonic, and the demon leaves. That's all right if the Holy Spirit does it.

That happened to Jesus, you know. He preached in the synagogue, and a man started screaming (Mark 1:23). Why? Because God came. God's presence caused an encounter with the demon; it was being flushed into the light. Jesus ministered in such a great anointing that it only took a few seconds, which I hope is where we are heading.

We must remember that the natural man cannot understand all the things of the Holy Spirit. I do not understand why God would do some of the things He does. You might ask, "Are you sure everything is totally God?" No, I am not. We are never going to have "pure God" in this life, are we? None of us reach perfection this side of heaven.

Remember, we need to have more faith in God's ability to bless us than in Satan's ability to deceive us.

As Guy Chevreau has so aptly said:

> What we see is always a mixture of flesh and Spirit. At times, some people may get a little goofy for God, and we'll see something like what Jonathan Edwards called "great imprudences and irregularities of conduct."
>
> But at least in my experience, it's far easier to correct and disciple someone who outsteps himself in fleshly zeal for the things of the Spirit, wanting more of God and getting a little silly in the process, than it is to try to work with someone who is carnally faultfinding and judgmental, especially when it comes to things of the Spirit. That's just as imprudent and irregular in terms of godliness — and often it's so very unteachable.

I would rather have that, too. I would rather have a

church like that — filled with the Spirit and the power of God — and we have one here now. But it's not perfect. Someone once commented, "If ever you find the perfect church, don't join it."

THE FRUIT OF THE PHENOMENA

I am well aware that when God's Spirit moves, the devil can counterfeit things. But what the devil cannot counterfeit is the work of grace that is done inside a person: the life-changing love affair with Jesus. That's why it's impossible to talk about the manifestations without talking about the fruit.

People who come to our meetings for the first time and watch may say to themselves, "What possible good could it do to fall down on the floor and lie there? What is that all about? Did it help them? Were they healed, or just what has happened exactly?"

We cannot judge what is happening inside a person by what we see happening on the outside. Remember, that would be like taking a photo of a man in the middle of a manifestation and saying, "This is bizarre and out of order. How can this be God?" No, instead we need a video of his life from that time on. How has his personal life with Christ been affected? How about his family? Do they notice any changes? What about at church or on the job?

We would not take a snapshot of Jesus chasing the moneychangers out of the temple — whip in hand, birds flying, animals scattering, money showering down (John 2) — and try to prove that He had no self-control.

Neither would we take a picture of the blind man with mud smeared on his eyes and say, "Is this ministry really from God?" No, we would say, "What happened as a result?" The point is that when he washed the mud off he could see, even though what happened seemed to violate acceptable religious protocol (John 9).

If you ask people who have been touched by God with

141

manifestations such as falling, laughter and shaking, they will have stories of intimate love to tell. Some would tell of anger released, some of oppression lifted, of joy and laughter breaking out of them — or just peace, peace, wonderful peace. Others would share visions or prophecies, for themselves or for the church. Most would say they have a fresh closeness to God.

If you had seen Camilla Douglas lying on the floor in our service, you would wonder how this is making a difference in her life. But if you talked to her afterward, she would tell you as she told us:

> I came over from Britain with one main desire — to know how much I was loved by Jesus Christ. I have been walking with Him for twenty years and have felt His power many times, but the cry of my heart was to know His love! Of course, I did know He loved me — because Christians know that! But somehow when I said it to someone, it barely convinced me, let alone them!
>
> On Thursday night, after an amazing session on the floor, I experienced the love and intimacy of Jesus in a mind-blowing way. Even on my own, whether at work or at home, I sense Jesus with me in the most beautiful way, which I pray will never go.

So many I have talked to say, "The manifestations and phenomena were worth it. They are not really the issue. I would not trade what God has done in me, my family and the church for anything in the world." They are just so excited about it.

Why does God do these things? Why do people shout out and fall down and shake, roll or laugh? I'm not 100 percent sure. Often they are reacting to the *power* that is going through them or the revelation being given to them in visions and dreams. People are seeing all kinds of glorious things, and their physical bodies are responding. They are excited about the fact that God in His grace has come.

We pray so long for God to come and revive us again. Then when He comes in power, because we do not understand everything, we fight against it and try to stop it. Have you ever heard of anything so stupid?

It used to take two to three years of teaching, counseling and praying with people to get a truth to move from their head to their heart. We would say, "God loves you." The Bible says, "God loves you." But until that truth gets into the heart, nothing changes. It is merely head knowledge. Yet we have seen the Holy Spirit take this truth from the head to the heart in minutes simply while people are lying out on the floor! I do not understand it all, but I know it's wonderful.

I am at the point where I say "God, come and blow our doors off. Lord, just come, let Your presence come, let it come, let it come. I welcome You." I cannot tolerate the way the church has been losing ground year after year. We are the laughingstock of the world — derided by the media, ridiculed by those in authority — but now things are changing. God is beginning to make us the head and not the tail. I like this a whole lot better.

There is another wave of the Spirit coming, and the people who get on board with this wave are going to love what is coming next. It will be a wave of great power. I cannot think of anything that would be more exciting than to say, "Let's go to the hospital this afternoon and empty it out." Wouldn't that be fantastic!

Lives are being changed for now, and here is the most wonderful part about renewal: the ministry of the Holy Spirit is being given back to ordinary people like you and me. Does that guarantee that we won't abuse it? Does that mean that some folks won't go off the edge one way or the other? No, but what we are seeing is this: The main body of Christians are flowing with the Father's blessing, getting healed themselves and then giving it away to others, again and again.

Our prayer for you is that you would not focus on the manifestations and phenomena. I want you to get past that quickly. Yes, they are biblical. Yes, the Holy Spirit does them, and yes they are wonderful. But the manifestations are not what we seek. If you come with humility of heart for the bread of heaven, the Holy Spirit is going to fill you and fill you with the reality of God. ☻

CHAPTER 10

THE PHENOMENA: REVELATIONS OF WHO GOD IS

The phenomena we see and hear in our services really grab people's attention. If you had heard nothing else about this new move of God before you picked up this book, you probably heard about the laughing, the shaking and the falling down.

That's why I am excited about having the opportunity to tell you about these unusual manifestations, especially as the people who have experienced them have come to understand them. Maybe you will learn to appreciate them as we do once you know what God is working out in the lives of individuals.

DRUNK IN THE SPIRIT

Why did people think the disciples were drunk on the day of Pentecost (Acts 2)? What were they acting like? They must have poured out of the upper room onto the streets. Maybe they staggered around as they declared the wonders of God in languages they did not know.

The people in Jerusalem heard the sound and crowded around the disciples. Some were amazed and awestruck, while others were disbelieving and critical, saying this could never be God.

"These men are not drunk, as you suppose" Peter informed them (Acts 2:15). The 120 disciples of Jesus had a wonderful day. That day the gift of God was given to them.

You know, God is full of surprises. He wants us to be happy, to enjoy His Spirit and His presence with us. Did you know that?

I received a letter from Pasteur Dave V. Vairogs of the Centre Évangélique de St. Hyacinthe Inc. in Ste-Rosalie, Québec in September 1994. He excitedly proclaimed, "There is revival here!" He described children and adults being "drunk" in the Spirit, laughing all night long. When they got up and were prayed for again, they went back down. This church has had to start a program to drive some of these people home after the services!

> Every time they go down, it's like they had another glass of booze, but it isn't that at all. It's the Lord's Spirit. If it was just limited to that, I guess that would not necessarily be special in and of itself, but it goes much, much further. While people are under the Spirit, they are delivered of all sorts of problems. They go to the heavenlies. They come back, and they are no longer the same. They are transformed.

Do not get drunk on wine, which leads to debauchery. Instead, be filled with the Spirit (Eph. 5:18).

Paul said that instead of being drunk with alcohol, which leads to excess, we should be filled with the Spirit. If we look at the original Greek, we discover that Paul is telling us, "Keep on continually being refilled with the Spirit." That gives new meaning to the verse, doesn't it? He implies that being filled with the Spirit will affect us somehow, yet the effect is desirable, and we should seek it repeatedly.

This is not a one-time experience, but rather something we should desire again and again. What does it look like when people are filled with the Spirit repeatedly? At times it looks like what happened on the day of Pentecost or in the house of Cornelius (Acts 10).

Occasionally people become so overcome with the Holy Spirit that they act and appear to be drunk. The first thing we need to say is that nothing in Scripture forbids us from being filled to capacity with the Holy Spirit. In fact, we are encouraged to be filled with Him. But would such a person appear to be drunk?

Jeremiah the prophet is so disturbed about the false prophets of Israel that in his continual prayer for the nation, he testifies to the following:

I am like a drunken man, like a man overcome by wine, because of the Lord and his holy words (Jer. 23:9).

Why are you like a drunken man, Jeremiah? "Because of the Lord and His holy words." Because of the Lord's presence and the words spoken to Jeremiah. Because of the effect of God on his life.

The surprising thing is that we do not react more when God comes in power. Perhaps being inebriated is getting off lightly, in response to His grace and love.

In *Mystical Phenomena*, Albert Farges wrote, "There are even more violent transports, such as those so often observed in St. Francis of Assisi, St. Philip Neri, St. Joseph of Cupertino, St. Mary Magdalene of Pazzi, and many other holy mystics, whose jubilation or spiritual inebriation showed itself outwardly in actions which astonished and even scandalized the weak and ignorant. Such were their sighs, cries, ardent and broken exclamations, abundant tears, and even laughter, songs, improvised hymns, tremors agitating every limb, leapings, impetuous movements, the violent outward expression of enthusiasm and love."[1]

Eddie Ensley wrote about drunkenness in the Spirit and holy laughter associated with jubilation throughout almost two millennia of church history. He wrote that St. Teresa of Avila likened "jubilation as a prayer that is supernatural and may last all day, and as a form of spiritual inebriation." She said, "It may last for a whole day, and the soul will then be like one who has drunk a great deal."[2] Much is being gleaned from church history and being documented and circulated at present that tells us over and over of similar manifestations both before and after the Reformation.

Being "drunk" in the Spirit sounds negative to many people, even though Paul implied that term. Maybe saying "joyously overcome by the Spirit" describes the experience better.

I've observed that the strong-willed, "cool," in-control type of people often find themselves drunk in the Spirit. I think it's God telling them that He's the boss, that He's an awesome God. It can be a humbling experience and makes one very vulnerable, but people are thrilled afterward because of the intimacy with God and changes of heart.

JOY AND LAUGHTER

When some people come into contact with the anointing of the Holy Spirit, they experience explosive joy and laughter. What is the purpose and benefit of holy laughter? My observations have been that intense laughter often accompanies emotional healing. People may laugh, then cry, then laugh. When asked later what they were going through, they tell of Jesus revealing hurts and healing them.

I have discussed this joy and laughter with Dr. John White, a psychiatrist from Vancouver, Canada. He observed that this new found joy so fortified and strengthened a person with the love of God that, in many cases, they were then able to deal positively with some very serious hurts and issues from their past. These Scriptures bear out this truth:

A happy heart makes the face cheerful, but heartache crushes the spirit (Prov. 15:13).

All the days of the oppressed are wretched, but the cheerful heart has a continual feast (Prov. 15:15).

A cheerful heart is good medicine, but a crushed spirit dries up the bones (Prov. 17:22).

Vic and Kathy Anfuso of Portland, Oregon, said they were "raised in the public eye and trained from birth to be dignified." They often heard the phrase, "They're watching." Now their friends are surprised to see them "on the floor doubled in laughter." They write, "As we yield our 'dignified' persons to God, He has given us a deeper freedom, worship, healing and intimacy. We know it is ever-growing as we are ever-yielding."

I remember a young mother in her late thirties named Julie who went home to Brighton, England, dancing. All she could do was walk on her toes the whole time she was at our meetings. I would say, "Julie, come here." And she would come tip-toeing over to me. I would ask, "Why are you walking on your toes?"

She would answer, "I don't know." She didn't know, but told how the Lord was speaking to her and saying "I want you to dance before Me." In the early seventies, when Julie was first baptized in the Holy Spirit, she had expressed herself in dance. But this had been quickly squashed by lack of understanding in fellow believers. The Holy Spirit was now restoring it.

Well, she went back to her family, and they thought it was really strange at first. But then they started to like it; it became fun. Later she wrote me, "This has brightened up our whole house. Everybody loves it. The Spirit of the Lord keeps falling on us, and we are having a great time loving Jesus as we have never loved Him before."

I saw Julie a year later. She was with her family, and they were all radiating the joy of the Lord.

FALLING

Prior to the renewal, we placed little value on people falling over. In fact, we used to say, "Hold them up." We were so anxious not to sensationalize anything that we almost went to the other extreme. Since then we have had to deal with the fact that thousands have fallen down and have arisen testifying to a wonderful work of grace. We set a high value on people receiving the things of the Spirit, and that often involves the manifestation of falling down. Yet we continue to emphasize the inward blessing.

Many people have had bad experiences with falling "under the power of God." Some, like myself, have previously been pushed or pulled or otherwise manipulated into falling down, so we try not to make falling down a big issue. It's similar to raising your hands during worship. It can facilitate intimacy with God.

Remember the first time you saw people worship with their hands in the air? You may have thought, "Boy, this is weird. I am not doing that." After a while you noticed that no one was paying any attention to you. You thought, "I wonder if it will help if I put my hands up?" So you looked around and put one hand up.

After a few weeks, you put both of them up, and it became no longer an issue for you. Now you worship the Lord with your hands up or with your hands down (Ps. 28:2; 63:4). It is immaterial; you are just worshiping Him.

What does it mean when people put their hands up? It means surrender; it means, "I am willing to be vulnerable." It lends itself to intimacy with God. Falling down is much the same. I believe God sees it as surrender to His lordship.

Also we have found that people are usually more comfortable lying down if they are going to be out any length of time. If they are sitting, they may slump over on someone else, and that person will become distracted. If people are lying on the floor, they are usually safer. It's as simple as that.

Carol and I were in Buffalo, New York, in September 1994 doing a program there with the TBN station. We had a great one-hour program, and afterward they wanted us to pray for the staff, so we did. They received prayer, and many were all over the floor laughing and crying. One lady was visiting, and I soaked her in prayer for five to ten minutes as she stood in front of me. Finally she opened her eyes and said, "I can't stand up any longer." I responded, "That is why people fall down." I love how Randy Clark responded once when asked why people fall down. He said, "It's because they can't stand up!"

If you want more information on this phenomena, Francis MacNutt, a former Catholic priest and well-known minister in North America, wrote a book called *Overcome by the Spirit* which goes through all the issues that are related to falling. It is most helpful.

Throughout the Word of God, people fall down when God

shows up. When He shows up a little, perhaps they have a say in the matter. But when He shows up a lot, they do not. They simply cannot stand up any longer, so they go down. The same thing is happening in this current move of God.

Throughout the Bible, we see instances of people falling down when they have a revelation of who God is. The soldiers came to arrest Jesus and asked which one He was. "I am He," Jesus replied, and they fell over backward to the ground (John 18:5-6).

When Solomon dedicated the temple, the cloud of God's presence came in, and the priests could not stand to minister (2 Chr. 5:14-15). Do you know what that means? If they could not stand because of the presence of God, then they fell.

The human body is just not geared to withstand this kind of power. That is why God allowed Moses only to look upon His glory after He had passed, but no one could look fully on Him and live (Ex. 33:20-23).

Jesus gave the apostle John a vision of the end times. John saw Jesus in all His glory (Rev. 1). Even in his vision, John fell down in the presence of the Lord.

Through the thousands of testimonies we've heard, we have discovered that when people fall, God often ministers to them in intimate, healing ways. But this amazing account shows us that falling in itself can produce fruit.

Ché Ahn, pastor of the Vineyard Christian Fellowship of Greater Pasadena, California, was speaking at a meeting at the Evangelical Formosan Church in San Diego. A young Chinese man named Allen was in the prayer line. He said, "I just want proof that God exists." So Ché said, "We'll pray that Jesus will make Himself more real to you." Without Ché even touching Allen, he went down to the ground. Then he immediately got back up and wanted to be prayed for again. Allen wanted to make sure what he just experienced was real.

This time Allen braced himself, and he went down again. When he got up this time, he said, "I want to give my life to Jesus Christ." They prayed together, then Allen said, "How can I get baptized?" Ché suggested meeting him tomorrow at his hotel and baptizing him in the swimming pool, but Allen wanted to get baptized immediately. So Ché got a Snapple bottle, rinsed and filled it with water, went to the restroom and drenched him!

God used this experience of falling under the power of God to show this young man that He was real.

Perhaps I should comment that there are those who say falling forward is biblical and of God, but falling backward is not. I find that Scripture records some falling forward, a few backward and many where it just does not say! We have witnessed the same person fall forward one time and backward another. The same positive fruit is evident in either case.

SHAKING

People often shake when the power of God hits them. Why are we so surprised that physical bodies react to God's power? It is a wonder to me that we do not explode and fly apart. God's power is real power — the *dunamis* of heaven.[3]

Suppose I handed you two bare electric wires and said, "Would you please hold these tightly? Take one in each hand and hold on while I plug it in." How many of you think you might shake a little bit? Can you imagine somebody saying at that moment, "Now, now, take it easy. You do not have to shake like that. You can take control of this thing. You can be quiet. You don't have to get all that excited."

A woman who had been with a campus ministry for five years came to our meetings in July 1994. She was burnt out with all the rejection she'd received from students. At first she could only cry when she got prayer, as she had for the three months previous. A few nights later, the leader spoke on fear. That struck a chord within her, and she went forward. She describes what happened:

> I was focusing on the cross and how Jesus' death and resurrection broke the power of death and the evil one. My right hand started mildly shaking. I lifted up specific fears to God (being passed by, rejection, not being used by God). Each time I prayed I increased in shaking till both arms were violently shaking. Then it was like really strong sparks or shocks were coming from my fingers, and I cried, "Oo, ow," continually.

Our team prayed for her, and after two hours, she started laughing with joy. The next day she said, "I feel lighter and free and eager to see what God will do when I go home."

People often don't shake at first. They lie still and gently receive. As the Lord starts to win their hearts, just as He did this woman's, they realize, "This is really You, Lord." They accept the experience because they trust that it is God. Their hearts open up, and He floods in. Often the experience with God becomes so powerful, they shake spontaneously.

Remember the prophet Daniel? He shook when He encountered the angel of the Lord (Dan. 10). Why was he trembling? It wasn't merely that he was afraid. God's power was on him. The God we serve is a very powerful God.

We may see a shaking-type manifestation, realizing it is something powerful, yet we never know what is really happening inside the person unless we ask him. Dick Schroeder, the campus ministry director in Montana, shared what was happening inside him while he was shaking.

As Steve (a fellow minister) prayed for a greater anointing, something unusual happened. I felt a twitch in my right arm. It twitched again and again. I was aware that I had a choice to make. Either I could yield to Jesus and trust Him or I could resist by holding my arm stiff. I chose to yield to Jesus.

My arm continued to twitch and flail for approximately ten minutes. That is what Steve saw. Internally, however, I was aware of something else. I saw Jesus come and take a sword that had already been in my hand and replace it with a larger sword. What appeared on the outside to be a flailing arm was actually the Holy Spirit teaching me to wield a bigger sword of spiritual authority.

Shaking for the most part is a person's response to the intense power of God going through the body. God's higher purposes are not usually obvious immediately. Many testify later to increased power and boldness to live the Christian life. We have often seen shaking accompany words of prophecy which were being given to individuals or congregations. The person shaking often has a heightened awareness of God's presence and therefore there is a release in faith and anointing.

OTHER ASTONISHING MANIFESTATIONS

Occasionally there are manifestations that we have never seen before. God says, "See, I am doing a new thing!" (Is. 43:19). They are intimately designed for that person.

A visitor from Essex, England, experienced a simple but lovely and unusual manifestation. Julian Reddihough told us he constantly smelled a beautiful perfume all around the conference hall and surroundings. He said, "I was told that all Christ's 'robes are fragrant with myrrh and aloes

155

and cassia'" (Ps. 45:8). What a beautiful and unexpected manifestation of God's presence.

I was sharing at a pastors' meeting in San Antonio in the fall of 1994, and the power of God came on a man from Venezuela. I knew in my spirit that he had been fasting, and it was later confirmed that he had just finished a forty-day fast. He was desperate for God. He was dressed in a double-breasted jacket and tie. It was hot in the room, but he wanted to dress right and be presentable. He was trying to take notes.

Suddenly the fire of God hit him. Away went his tie, away went his jacket, away went his notes. I think his shoes even came off. He was so on fire, we thought he was going to explode. We said, "Lord, thank You for touching him. Please give him more." The man started jumping up in the air and shouting, "My feet are on fire! My feet are on fire." He was leaping about and didn't know what to do. Finally he ran around the room shaking his head and saying, "My hands are on fire; I am on fire."

The next night we had another meeting, and the same thing happened — the Holy Spirit came on him again with fire. He was leaping, jumping, running and stomping his feet. He felt so on fire that he took his shoes off and ran faster.

His precious wife was three months pregnant, and she started shouting, "The baby inside me is jumping." Carol put her hand on the woman's stomach, and it felt like the baby was jumping, jumping, jumping. The baby seemed to feel God's fire as well. This mother was so thrilled. It was the first time she felt the baby move. She said, "This is what happened to Elizabeth when Mary arrived and the Holy Spirit touched John while he was still in the womb."

This couple shared that the love they felt from Christ was overwhelming. They received what they came to God for. The Holy Spirit changed that man right before our eyes. He fell in love with Jesus — passionately and excitedly. It was not just refiner's fire; it was the passion of romance that came into his and his wife's heart. They were totally transformed in an instant by the love and the fire of God.

I watched him after the meeting in the hotel lobby. He was excitedly telling unbelievers that Jesus had just come on him with the fire of God. People were saying, "OK, OK. Stay away from me." He thought I had something to do with it. He kept thanking me, but I said, "It's Him. It's Jesus. He really loves you; I am just the delivery boy."

HEALINGS

When we think of healings, we think of physical healings. And we have definitely seen physical healings. But so far in this renewal we have seen many more inner healings. You have already read several testimonies about these.

Many wonder about the value of inner healing today. Wasn't everything completed at the cross? Why then do we need further works of grace? It is often assumed that all our problems can be solved through the Christian disciplines alone, and that we must use our self-discipline to see us through the further works of sanctification. At one time I even felt that to suggest the need for further works of grace was to imply that the finished work of Christ on the cross was insufficient. This, of course, is not the case.

Multitudes of Christians, however, are not leading victorious Christian lives. One of the leading reasons for this is deep emotional wounds from the past which have left them struggling to stay afloat. These people are prisoners of their own broken hearts.

> The Spirit of the Sovereign Lord is on me, because
>   the Lord has anointed me to preach good news
>   to the poor.
> He has sent me to *bind up the brokenhearted,* to
>   proclaim freedom for the captives and release

157

from darkness for the prisoners (Is. 61:1, italics added).

Is it not just like Jesus to come and rescue His wounded lambs, to bind up their hurts and fill them with inexpressible joy? That is inner healing at its best. The sovereign Lord comes and heals people inside so they no longer focus most of their energy inward in a "poor me" survival mode, but they are now glad to be alive and looking for ways to bless others. Manifold testimonies declare this to be true.

Pastor John Overholt wrote me about an inner healing God did in him. He was resting in the Lord and was taken back to a baseball game he played in when he was fourteen years old. It was his final game of the season and a special one because his dad was in the stands watching for the first time all season. John did what all kids dream of — he scored the winning run while his dad was watching — and he was thrilled. John continues:

> As the Lord brought this all to mind, I realized that I had a deep-rooted hurt in my life over the lack of time spent between my dad and me. Then the Father spoke a truth into my heart that set me free.
>
> "John," He said, "I was at every one of your games. I saw every strikeout and every hit. I was there all the time."
>
> With that simple revelation, it was like a dam of hurt just crumbled and rivers of joy came gushing forth. I was overcome with laughter well into the evening because I was so liberated by the simple revelation that my heavenly Father had time for me.

This is the Father's blessing to us — healing the broken-hearted, binding up our wounds. What a loving heavenly Father we have! He wants to heal us inside and out.

Aryanne Oade of London, England, suffered from back problems most of her life. At an early age she was thrown from a horse and later in her teens had endured an injury to her neck playing soccer, which added to her problems and pain. She went through years of therapy, medication and doctor visits. Her muscles and bones seemed fixed "out of shape," and she had to be careful not to move about or stretch too much.

In October 1994, she went to see Sarah Bright, a Christian osteopath. During that first talk Aryanne saw how certain life issues, which God had been helping her with, were inextricably linked to her back problems. These issues were largely borne out of pain and fear which had caused her to physically and emotionally curl up inside herself. Sarah prescribed exercises which began to help.

That next February Aryanne came to Holy Trinity Brompton in London where I was speaking. At the end of the night, I asked if anyone wanted prayer for physical healing, so she came up. When I prayed for her, she told me she felt a warmth traveling up and down her spine. The second time I put my hand on her head, she fell over and was out in the Spirit for a short time, during which she felt a realigning in her pelvis.

When Aryanne got up off the floor she started to prod the joint in her lower back which had been so painful. She said touching this joint used to produce a sick pain, but now she felt no pain. She pressed all the surrounding areas. Still, no pain. Aryanne felt very excited but refused to leap to any conclusions, sticking to what she knew for sure — at that moment there was no pain. Several days later her osteopath examined her and pronounced:

> I've never seen anything like it. You have a model back. Your pelvis is no longer anteriorly rotated. In all the places where the ligaments were soggy,

they are now strong. The Lord has done me out of a job.

Since then Aryanne has had no pain whatsoever in her back or neck. She testifies:

> I now routinely do movements which I would not have contemplated doing before. I have no fear of overstretching or hurting myself, and I feel a strength in my back that is new and reassuring. I move about with complete freedom. My posture is no longer marked by an S-shaped stoop. My pelvis sits where it should, without the backward tilt it once had.
>
> I've seen God repair me emotionally, and as He has taken fear and pain out of me, physical healing has come.

So we see that God heals emotionally and physically, and in Aryanne's case, they were related.

One remarkable physical healing we witnessed involved a young girl. Thirteen-year-old Heather Harvey from Kentucky was prayed for in one of our meetings. Heather has had dyslexia all her life. She was totally out for an hour. When she got up, she told the amazing story of a vision she saw while out under God's power.

She had been on an operating table in a cold room. (Her mother tells us that Heather has never been in the hospital and wouldn't have known that operating rooms are cold.) Angels were doing brain surgery on her, making connections in her brain. She heard God orchestrating the surgery. Heather then had a second vision of going back home and praying for her friends who had dyslexia.

After this experience, Heather could immediately read better and didn't mix up her letters when she typed. When she got home, she prayed for her friend, Monica

Morgan-Dohner, who then fell out and had a similar vision of angels working on her brain, "pulling out parts that were dented in." But Heather hadn't told Monica yet about her own "angelic surgery." Afterward, Monica's tutor said she no longer has dyslexia. Now these girls will pray for anyone who has dyslexia, anywhere, anytime.[4]

Since physical healings were so much a part of the ministry of Jesus, I believe that we will see many more of them as renewal turns into revival. Healings will be one of the things that fuel multitudes of conversions.

VISIONS

Saul was a very religious Pharisee who went to Damascus to arrest the followers of Jesus. He was a servant of Jehovah, and he wanted to stomp out this new "cult" that had arisen.

> As he neared Damascus on his journey, suddenly a light from heaven flashed around him. He fell to the ground and heard a voice say to him, "Saul, Saul, why do you persecute me?"
>
> "Who are you, Lord?" Saul asked.
>
> "I am Jesus, whom you are persecuting," he replied. "Now get up and go into the city, and you will be told what you must do" (Acts 9:3-6).

The men traveling with Saul heard the sound, but saw no one. Saul had been knocked to the ground by the power of God, and when he got up and opened his eyes, he was blind. Ananias, a disciple of Jesus, had to pray for him so Saul could receive his sight again.

Let's bring this into the twentieth century. Suppose that one day a man who is known as religious, very zealous, eager for God and very legalistic, comes to church. Suddenly he is on the ground, and people heard something, but they do not know what to think. He says, "I have seen a vision and

161

heard a voice," and yet he is blind when he gets up off the floor. What will you tell his mother?

Later this same man, now named Paul, writes about other "visions and revelations from the Lord" he has had. He admits he didn't know if he was in his body or apart from his body when he had them. But he was caught up to "the third heaven" and "paradise" (2 Cor. 12).

When Mahesh Chavda, a delightful and well known evangelist from Florida, visited our church, he had a vision one night in his hotel room. He saw Carol and me come to him. I prayed for him, saying, "More, Lord," while Carol touched his feet. He was shaking. The bed was shaking, and Mahesh was afraid it would wake his wife, Bonnie. During this time, he received some wonderful encouraging words for Carol and me.

Mahesh's description of this sounds like Paul's: "It was a dream, a vision — I do not know. But it was in the realm of the Spirit, and it was so real."

On the day of Pentecost the apostle Peter explained, quoting from the prophet Joel, that people in the last days would experience visions and dreams (just as Paul did).

> In the last days, God says, I will pour out my Spirit on all people. Your sons and daughters will prophesy, your young men will see visions, your old men will dream dreams. Even on my servants, both men and women, I will pour out my Spirit in those days, and they will prophesy. I will show wonders in the heavens above and signs on the earth below, blood and fire and billows of smoke (Acts 2:17-19).

What we've had so far is only the introduction. We've seen visions and we've had prophecies, but we haven't seen blood and fire and billows of smoke. But it's coming.

CAROL'S VISION

Our church prayed for Carol and me before we went on an outreach trip to Eastern Europe in February 1994. She fell down on the platform. We saw her hands and feet moving, and every now and then her feet went up into the air and she made running movements. Then she lay quietly again until she repeated the actions. We were wondering what was happening to her. Later she related the vision she had — it was her first.

> As I was lying there, I felt the presence of the Lord come on me. Suddenly I saw this beautiful meadow with all kinds of flowers scattered in it. I wondered where this was. Jesus came by and handed me a bouquet of lilies of the valley, which have a special meaning to me because John gave me some years ago when I was going through a very difficult time. The Lord had told me then, "Carol, lilies of the valley only grow in the valley. They do not grow on the mountain tops. When you go through the valleys of life, you need to find the lilies that I have placed there for you." They were a reminder of His faithfulness during life's darkest hours.
>
> In the vision, Jesus and I skipped along and talked heart-to-heart. We began to run and play and have a wonderful, intimate time together. As we were sharing, He stopped and said, "May I have the bouquet back?" I said, "Oh, OK," and I reluctantly handed the bouquet back to Him. He went around and gathered all different colored flowers — red, purple, white and yellow — and formed them into a floral wreath. He then wove the lilies of the valley into the wreath and put it on

my head. I watched as He attached a very long, white wedding veil to the wreath.

The scene changed, and I was walking, holding His arm. I kept looking around thinking, "Gee, I don't recognize this place. I wonder where I am? This doesn't look familiar at all." Then I happened to look down, and I thought, "Oh, it's gold! Oh, my goodness, I am walking on the streets of gold. This is heaven! I'm the bride of Christ. I am marrying Jesus. This is the wedding day. Lord, this is incredible."

What happened next tenderly reminded me how personal the Lord is to each one of us. When I get discouraged or weighed down by life's business, I like to go see baby calves or colts or other animals, and it fills and refreshes me. I have always said, "Oh Lord, I can hardly wait to get to heaven so I can hug a tiger." I want to put my face right in it's fur and give it a big hug.

As the vision proceeded, along the way all these animals were there, and they were all bright and chipper. There were tigers and lambs and baby colts — and even my two pet dogs. It really blessed me.

Then the scene changed again, and we were in a huge room. Table after table after table was laid out with linen and crystal and silverware as far as the eye could see. There were candelabras and beautiful floral arrangements and the most gorgeous platters of food, like something you would see at a king's coronation — absolutely gourmet and elegant. I realized that this must be the wedding feast. "I married You, and this must be the banquet." I marveled. "But I don't see anybody, Lord. Where is everybody?"

As I turned around, I saw many people. They were absolutely gorgeous, attired in the most incredible wedding gowns you have ever seen. Their faces were glowing and I said, "Oh, Lord, who are these people?" He answered, "They are the naked and the outcasts and the wretched and the downtrodden and the broken. I have compelled them to come into My wedding feast."

I was standing in an open spot when Jesus walked up and said, "Carol, may I have the first dance?" I thought, "Oh, no, I can't dance. My wedding veil is too long." As soon as I thought that, out of nowhere came cardinals and blue jays — all these little birds — and they picked up my veil, and I danced with Jesus.

I later found out that while I way lying on the platform, my friend Shirley Smith came and began to sing over me. But in my vision, it was Jesus singing to me. He was singing that I was His treasure, His chosen one; He sang all the scriptures He had spoken to my heart when I was first converted.

When the vision finished, I thought, "Wow, Lord. Was that just for me? It could not just be all for me?" He said. "I want you to get up and share the vision with the people. When you have finished, I want you to tell them that My wedding feast is almost prepared — it is almost ready. Tell them that they are not to be like the five foolish virgins, but they are to be like the five wise virgins."

"This is a time that I am pouring out My Spirit," He continued. "I am pouring out the oil they can buy, and they can be filled and filled and filled. This is the time for My church and My bride to be filled with the oil of My Spirit. When they become filled, I will spill them out into the highways and byways. I will spread them all over, and they will not have to evangelize like they used to. Being so filled with My Spirit will compel the naked and the wretched and the broken to come in to My kingdom. Then I will come for them."

I thank the Lord that this experience was so intimate, precious and life changing for Carol. Not only did it bless her immensely, but retelling it has blessed thousands of people. The wonderful revelatory and prophetic edge to visions such as this strengthens, encourages and comforts the body of Christ (1 Cor. 14:3).

May the Lord again visit His people with many visions and dreams and remind us how glorious the kingdom is. May He come on us now and increase His signs and wonders among us and give us glorious revelations to our hearts.

THE FATHER'S BLESSING IS FOR EVERYONE

The physical and outward signs, although part of the package, are not what we seek. I don't care if you fall down or not. I don't care if you laugh, cry or shake. What I care about is that you are impacted heart-to-heart by the Holy Spirit's power. When that happens there is life-changing fruit produced in your life. I thank God for so many new Christians who have started their Christian life experiencing the power of God — we have had well over five thousand to date. What a privilege to begin with a profound revelation of God's love.

Purpose in your heart to receive a fresh outpouring of the Holy Spirit right now. God is fulfilling the promises of Joel 2:28-30 all over the world, in every nation and in every denomination. The Spirit is being poured out on all flesh! Begin to seek God earnestly for more. He is filling the

hungry with good things, but the rich (those already satisfied) He sends away empty (Luke 1:53).

One of the best places to receive more from the Lord is
right in your own home. Begin to spend quality time with
Him. Love Him. Worship Him. Ask, seek, knock and you
will receive.

Sometimes it is helpful to have others you trust pray for
you with the laying on of hands. Find a meeting nearby
where the fire of God is burning and go catch the fire. We
encourage people coming to our church in Toronto to
come for at least three days so they can "soak" in the presence of God. We want to marinate them in the Holy Spirit.
As this happens, they invariably experience a time of
refreshing from above.

Set aside your busy schedule. Give God a few days of
intimate time and soak in His presence. Do whatever it
takes, but don't miss the blessing the Father has for you!❂

CHAPTER 11

THE PROPHETIC: ANIMAL SOUNDS AND INSIGHTS

I couldn't believe what I was hearing. "Did you say someone roared in the meeting last night?" I repeated. I was in St. Louis with Randy Clark about five months into this renewal, and I had called to see how things were going at home.

"The meetings are going great," I was told. "Oh, and someone roared like a lion last night."

I was shocked. "Did he hurt anyone? Was it demonic? Did he attack anybody?"

"No."

"Well," I asked, "did you stop him?"

"No. We felt it was from the Lord."

I was dumbfounded. "Please, Lord. It has been so wonderful up to now," I whispered to God. "Don't let it go weird."

When I arrived back in Toronto later that week, the man who had roared was still at our meetings. I interviewed him in the front of the church. He was Gideon Chiu, a prominent Cantonese Chinese leader from Vancouver, Canada, a pastor's pastor, very honored and well-respected.

He shared what he was feeling and how he had come to Toronto desperately hungry for more of God. Suddenly this meek and mild pastor started roaring again, right in front of everyone. He moved back and forth across the front of our church, roaring and lunging like an angry lion, crying, "Let My people go! Let My people go!"

Then he came back to the microphone and testified that the Chinese people have been deceived by the dragon for hundreds of years, but now the Lion of the tribe of Judah was coming to set His people free. Our church immediately exploded into volumes of praise as they bore witness to what the Spirit of God was saying.

Since that night, we have occasionally seen and heard what has come to be called "animal sounds" in our church. As I've observed this phenomena, I've come to some conclusions.

FACTS ABOUT ANIMAL SOUNDS

The first thing you need to know about the animal sounds in our meetings is that they are very rare. We can go for a week or more with none occurring, and fifteen hundred people attend nightly meetings here six nights a week.

The next critical fact to know is that the people who have had these peculiar manifestations are for the most part largely credible leaders. They are usually people who are tried and proven in ministry or people of spiritual integrity whom I — or others — have known for a long time. They have hearts for the lost and have cried out to God for the nations.

Third, you need to know that these sounds are most often made in the context of prophecy, vision and revelation.

They usually occur after lots and lots of soaking prayer. We don't have the time or ministry team members to do this volume of praying with many people. I believe this is better suited for a private place with trusted friends. Yet, sometimes God allows them to occur in public meetings for everyone to see and contemplate.

THE PROPHETIC WORD — ACTED OUT

Assuming these sounds are prompted by the Holy Spirit, what could He possibly be doing?

Prophecies from God can be about the future — what He has in store for us or for the world — or words of building up and encouragement for the body of Christ.

> Surely the Sovereign Lord does nothing without revealing his plan to his servants the prophets (Amos 3:7).

Either this is true or it isn't, and since we believe the Bible, we believe this is true. There are still prophetic people around who hear the word of the Lord, and He wants to reveal His plan to His servants.

The gift of prophecy is for the New Testament church.

> Follow the way of love and eagerly desire spiritual gifts, especially the gift of prophecy...everyone who prophesies speaks to men for their strengthening, encouragement and comfort...prophecy, however, is for believers, not for unbelievers (1 Cor. 14:1,3,22).

We were used to words of prophecy given in the conventional manner — someone prompted by the Holy Spirit speaking out in a church service. If someone in your church gave a prophecy which started, "I am coming like a roaring lion to deliver My children," would people accept it? Yes, they would test it by the Word, and if it agreed, they would accept it with joy.

What if God chose to have someone act out the prophecy — complete with sound effects — in addition to speaking the words? It is likely that the message would stay with people; they would not forget it before the service was over. In this manner, I've observed that animal sounds are often part of an intense acted-out prophecy.

This idea of showing instead of just telling should not seem foreign to us. Jesus took advantage of situations to show, not only tell, His disciples truths. He called a child to stand before them, then told His followers they had to change and become as children to enter the kingdom of heaven (Matt. 18:1-6). He broke bread to teach them about the sacrifice of His broken body for them (Matt. 26:26-29). He cursed the fig tree and it immediately withered to illustrate the power of faith (Matt. 21:19).

God often had prophets of the Old Testament act out messages to His people. For example, the Lord told Isaiah to strip, take off his sandals and go around like that for three years. God explains why.

> Just as my servant Isaiah has gone stripped and barefoot for three years, as a sign and portent against Egypt and Cush, so the king of Assyria will lead away stripped and barefoot the Egyptian captives and Cushite exiles (Is. 20:4-5).

Sometimes God chooses to show us things instead of telling us with words.

When people in a meeting act like or make sounds like

an animal as part of a prophetic word from God, afterward they will tell us how empowered they felt during the prophecy. Often they feel great strength going into them, perhaps similar to Samson's anointing for strength.

I can just imagine what sort of noises Samson made when the Spirit of God came on him and he carried the city gates to the top of the hill. I doubt he said, "Oh well, let's do this quietly." Empowered by God's Spirit (Judg. 16:3), he probably made a great roar in the middle of the night as he tore the posts out of the ground and carried them to the top of the hill.

The atmosphere surrounding these manifestations is often one of confrontation — a warfare mode of aggressively defeating the enemy or explosively displaying God's wrath. Part of the bravado that goes along with any battlefield scenario is all the yelling and noise. It is a natural impulse when people are going to war. If people are fighting hand-to-hand with swords, there's going to be yelling. I think that is an impartation of power and strength, and a declaration of war. When these manifestations occur there is often the intensity of a warrior accompanying them.

ROARING OF A LION

Perhaps the reason that the roaring of a lion has been the predominant prophetic sound we've heard is that Jesus is coming back in triumph. He was already the sacrificed Lamb; the next time we see Him, it will be as the victorious King — the Lion of Judah.

In Revelation, we see the Lamb taking the scrolls to open them and initiate the pouring out of God's wrath on the world during the end time. As John is watching, an elder explains, "See, the Lion of the tribe of Judah, the Root of David, has triumphed. He is able to open the scroll and its seven seals" (5:5).

Jesus is returning soon as the victorious Lion of Judah.

172

The lion has roared — who will not fear?
The Sovereign Lord has spoken — who can but
prophesy? (Amos 3:8).

In this scripture Amos makes a direct comparison
between God speaking and the lion roaring — and people
prophesying. The prophecies we hear in our church that
are associated with roaring often do reveal God's plans.

I have never roared like a lion. I do not know for sure
exactly why it occurs, but I think the most valuable way to
approach this phenomena is to ask the people who have
done it what happened, what they were seeing and feeling
within and how it affected their lives. They will invariably
give us helpful insights.

Senior Pastor Byron Mote of Eaglemount Family Ministries
in Lewisville, Texas, had an unexpected experience with
roaring. At a pastor's meeting in Lewisville, this very proper
pastor in a starched pink shirt with a nice tie was roaring
and walking around like a lion in front of two hundred
other pastors. He said he was thinking, "O Lord, please do
not let this get out of hand. Please, no; I don't understand
this."

A similar experience happened to him the following
night. Later Byron told us of the vision he was seeing at the
time.

> An army was marching against the gates of hell,
> which surrounded the city [of Lewisville, Texas].
> We seemed to march for a long time before we
> approached the iron gates. As we came in range
> of the gates, the demons sitting on the gates began
> to shoot their fiery darts at us. They cast darts of
> greed, lust, pride, independence, religion, power
> — all the weapons that had worked so well before.
> However, this time they had no effect. In fact, they
> only seemed to strengthen that army. God said,

"What Satan means for harm, I will use for good."

During this time my wife, Jan, was praying at my feet, and John's wife, Carol, at my head. Jan was having a vision of marking off the city, and I was marching around those blocks to claim them for Jesus. Just as the Lord said, "It is finished, the city is Mine," I let out the roar of the lion, and she saw the demons flee from the city.

As we got right in front of the wall, I heard the Commander-in-Chief say, "Roar, Judah, roar." I let out several loud roars while lying on the floor as I continued swinging my arms and moving my legs in a marching motion. As I did, I saw the gates of hell vanish! They did not fall down; they just vanished! I then saw the people of the city on the other side. It was as if their eyes were opened and they could see spiritually for the first time. I heard them say, "Ahhh, this is the true church and there is the Lord."

I said, "Lord, why have they not repented?" He said, "You must now travail and cry out for them to repent. I have opened their eyes, now travail for them." I asked, "How do we do this?"

The Lord explained Byron's roaring to him as he lay resting in the Spirit on the first night.

"The roar is as the cry of My people for the lost. Many have prayed for the harvest, but it is not with a broken heart; it is to build churches. Until My church cries out for the lost with such fervency and purity that I will hear it as the roar of the Lion, they will not see the harvest.

My people must cry out as desperately as Israel cried out for deliverance from Egypt. My people must cry out as desperately as a parent would cry out for a dying child. They must see and hear the reality of hell. They must lie broken and weeping for the lost. This is the heart that I am looking for. These are the people who will stand in the gap for the lost."

The second night, as Byron lay on the floor, the Lord told him how the travail would come. He said that this recent move of the Spirit is the Lord romancing His church. Then His church would become spiritually "with child," conceiving a deep burden for the lost. He said this could not occur by natural means, but must come from Him. Then His church will labor in prayer to bring forth the harvest of souls.

I told the Lord, "I love the vision, but couldn't You have given it to him a little...you know, differently?"

But those types of visions necessarily go along with an outpouring of power. Byron then got up and started praying over other people who were lying on the floor. He says:

> During this time I realized that the physical and strange manifestations were often prophetic. I would begin to pray over people who had strong manifestations and God would show me what was happening. Sometimes He would tell me to prophesy over them. Not only did this seem to increase the manifestation, but it also brought understanding to those who were watching. Now, instead of this just being strange or possibly even a "turnoff," it brought meaning to what was happening.

Incidentally, pastors from different churches in the Lewisville area are now meeting together to pray. There are weekly renewal meetings with twelve to fifteen churches involved. Byron notes, "The army is being formed and beginning the march on the city. The churches are sanctifying themselves to resist the fiery darts of the enemy."

I saw this in August of 1995 at a Catch the Fire conference in Dallas, Texas. It was a powerful time together, and the meetings were sponsored by local pastors. Byron's vision is starting to be fulfilled.

Others have had reservations about the animal noises made in our services. John Moore from Montana had previously heard demonic spirits make a wide range of noises including sounds of animals. He came to Toronto with some caution. The third night he was there the Holy Spirit came upon him powerfully. He says:

> I was soon on my hands and knees crawling on all fours with visions of lions running through my head.
>
> At one point I definitely sensed the Spirit suggesting I roar. I did not, thinking it would be best to test the spirits. Perhaps I tested them too long, for soon I realized I was meant to roar but had been disobedient.
>
> Although His presence stayed upon me mightily for at least another hour, the inclination to roar never returned. I tried to stir it up (not mimic it) a time or two and felt rebuked by the Lord each time.
>
> Any manifestation of God is wrong when it is copied in the flesh, but there is absolutely no doubt in my mind that the anointing on me to roar was from God.

John said he had missed a blessing by being overly cautious.

The Bible says the Lord will roar out like a lion and His children will follow Him (Hos. 11:10). When that happens will we, His children, be overly cautious and miss His blessing?

Lion, Ox, Man and Eagle

Some people say that since human beings are made in the image of God, making animal sounds is degrading; therefore, the Holy Spirit would never be behind them. Yet God Himself had no hesitation in describing Himself using animals that symbolized certain characteristics. Jesus is not only called the Lamb that was slain from the foundation of the world (1 Pet. 1:19-20; Rev 13:8), but also the Lion of the tribe of Judah (Rev. 5:5).

In the very throne room of heaven, we see animals used in the descriptions of the four living creatures who constantly worship God.

> In the center, around the throne, were four living creatures, and they were covered with eyes, in front and in back. The first living creature was like a lion, the second was like an ox, the third had a face like a man, the fourth was like a flying eagle. Each of the four living creatures had six wings and was covered with eyes all around, even under his wings. Day and night, they never stop saying:
>
> "Holy, holy, holy is the Lord God Almighty, who was, and is, and is to come" (Rev. 4:6-8).

These living creatures are covered with eyes. They have eyes in the back of their head, under their wings, over their wings and everywhere else. What does that mean? They can really see, which probably signifies they have prophetic ability. I believe this is an indication of the high value God puts on the gift of prophecy.

God wants a prophetic church. He tells us to seek the gift

of prophecy (1 Cor. 14:1). Moses wished that all the Lord's people were prophets and that the Lord would put His Spirit on them all (Num. 11:29). Again in Joel 2:28 as the Spirit is outpoured, there is much prophecy.

Many theologians believe that these four living creatures who worship God continually also represent the different ministries of Jesus: The lion — king over all; the ox — faithful, hard-working servant; the eagle — prophetic, visionary; and man — Jesus as the Son of Man.

It is no coincidence that we have seen people prophetically acting like lions, oxen, eagles and even warriors. In Steve Witt's church in St. Johns, New Brunswick, I saw all four of those manifestations happening at the same time — the ox, the eagle, the lion and the man (warrior). The lion and eagle manifestations accompanied prophesying. The man who was acting out the part of the warrior had both hands gripped together around the hilt of a sword, and he was swinging it. These warrior actions give the observer a real feel of battlefield action. The people who were doing this were mostly credible pastors or leaders. I was astonished but sensed the awesome presence of God.

One lady who played keyboard and weighed about 115 pounds was on all fours, snorting and pawing the ground like an angry ox or bull. It was obvious that she was surprised and a bit frightened by what was happening, but at the same time she seemed determined to follow the Spirit's leading.

For about an hour and a half this lady gave the most incredible prophetic word. She expressed the anger of the Lord against what Satan has done to God's church, His people, His cities and communities. She said the powers of darkness were being pushed back and new boundaries were being set.

Since that meeting, the pastor of the church says significant breakthroughs have taken place in their city. Many

teenagers have come to Christ. The church is moving powerfully in renewal. In addition, the woman who gave this
prophecy has since grown in Christ very significantly. Now
she is an encouraging prophetic voice in that church.

When people see this, their first inclination is to say,
"This is demonic." Remember, that's how I reacted, too.
This is too simplistic a view, however. Our past experiences
with demonic manifestations is that they will try to attack
those attempting to minister to the person. We know these
animal sounds and manifestations are not demonic because
we have never been attacked by anyone. The anger of the
Lord shown through the people making these sounds is
often directed toward the works of darkness. The works of
Satan are being torn down by God through this, not built
up.

I do not deny that sometimes it could be the flesh. Every
now and then somebody on the fringe did not get what he
came for and will try to fake something. We had one guy
imitating the roaring of the lion. I had to tell him, "Stop
doing that. You are too broken. You need your heart healed
first." I suggested to him to listen to some of John and Paula
Sandford's teaching tapes on inner healing.

If you, as a pastor or leader, know the person's heart,
integrity and reputation and they are in your fellowship,
you are much more able to discern the situation. You will
realize it is most probably the Holy Spirit empowering the
person, not the flesh or the demonic.

Keep in mind, too, that all prophecy — acted out or spoken
— needs to be tested (1 Cor. 14:29). We need to judge it by
these standards:

1. Is it scriptural?
2. Does it glorify Jesus?
3. Does it edify, exhort or
   comfort the body of Christ?

We've seen and heard many prophecies that relate to what God is doing on earth today and will do in the coming days.

PROPHECIES OF GOD'S COMING WRATH

The Lord is going forth like a warrior today.

> The Lord will march out like a mighty man, like a warrior he will stir up his zeal; with a shout he will raise the battle cry and will triumph over his enemies.

> "For a long time I have kept silent, I have been quiet and held myself back.
> But now, like a woman in childbirth, I cry out, I gasp and I pant.
> I will lay waste the mountains and hills and dry up all their vegetation.
> I will turn rivers into islands and dry up the pools.
> I will lead the blind by ways they have not known, along unfamiliar paths I will guide them;
> I will turn the darkness into light before them and make the rough places smooth.
> These are the things I will do; I will not forsake them" (Is. 42:13-16).

We have seen God going forth like a warrior in a prophetic context. People who are under a powerful anointing will stand and shout and yell as though they were full of anger as we continue to soak them in prayer and ask for more.

The first time I saw this happen, it intimidated me. A big, strong youth leader was yelling and shouting like an angry warrior. I thought, "Dear Lord, I hope this is You. Please let this be You, Holy Spirit, because if this is demonic, we are going to need about ten men in a hurry." But it was the Lord; He was venting His anger and His fury through one of His people. It was a statement — a powerful, powerful statement. God was announcing His intentions to move powerfully over the earth.

I tell you God is angry at the way the world has become. He is angry about so many starving children, motherless and fatherless teenagers, homeless people and those without hope. He is angry about crime and drug and alcohol abuse. It is because of demonic greed and sin, and He is angry about it all.

Also, it should not surprise any of us that we do not always understand what God is doing. Make sure it is God by evaluating it as I have explained, and then trust Him. Sometimes in His mercy He lets us in on what is happening and what it is all about. Often He'll tell us later, but not knowing everything is part of what being a little child is all about.

OTHER MANIFESTATIONS

The Holy Spirit has come to bring incredible glory to Jesus. He wants the power of the kingdom of God back on the face of the earth, and He is doing it like a lion with power and authority. Renewal is going forth like a wildfire everywhere, and these peculiar manifestations are a part of it.

Carole Baerg is a registered nurse from the Toronto area who has been coming to our meetings since the beginning. One day I asked her teasingly, "Carol, have you roared yet?" She said, "No, but I have crowed like a rooster."

I thought, "Oh no, Lord. Why did I ask her?" Then I said to her, "Because I know your heart and that you love Jesus, I know you would never be swept away by emotionalism. You are pressing into God as you never have in your life; you've been healed physically and emotionally, and you are just not the same person. Have you any idea what it meant?"

Her answer shocked me. She said, "Yes, I know exactly what it meant. There is a new day coming."

I thought, "I should have figured that out." God moves creatively but so simply.

There is a call going out today to "eat" His flesh and drink His blood, to partake of who Jesus really is to find out about His kingdom of love, and to let the love of God come in and be the answer. If this and some of the accounts I have been sharing offend you, then maybe they were designed to. We have found most of them to be God.

GOD WILL OFFEND YOUR MIND TO REVEAL YOUR HEART

John Wimber preached a message several years ago in the context of prophetic ministry that really impacted me: *God will offend your mind to reveal your heart.*

What sort of things offend us? Things about the way the church is? The way the world is? The way our own hearts are? The things that offend us reveal our inner hearts — and there we often find considerable unbelief.

When we counsel people, we often look at the things that make them angry. That's because our angers are windows into our hearts. When we explore why we overreact to something, we discover the deeper issues or hurts that need to be addressed.

The same dynamic happens when our minds are offended. We need to ask ourselves why, then peer into that window which reveals the heart. Maybe it shows us past hurts or the fear of losing control. Whatever it is, knowing about it is the first step toward change.

When I heard John preach this message, I had to say, "Lord, my heart is so full of unbelief about prophecy. But I know it is biblical; I do not want unbelief to be there."

When I explored why I was afraid of prophecy, I realized

it was because I had seen it misused. Words spoken in truth but without love had injured people, leaving them exposed and wounded. Understanding this allowed me to choose to trust God again with the gift of prophecy.

Our minds are constantly being offended by the things that God is doing, just as Jesus' words and actions offended the minds of the people in His day.

OUR RESPONSE

Critics have talked about the manifestations and animal sounds so much that they have been blown out of proportion. I have had to spend large and disproportionate amounts of time discussing and explaining them. One day I said to God, "This has been such a wonderful renewal, Lord. If only You hadn't brought in these animal sounds and this strange prophecy." The Lord responded, "Would you like Me to take it away?"

After contemplating for a few moments I had to say, "No, Lord. I want all that You have for us — even what I don't fully understand. I want to be humble and willing to be humbled. You are the sovereign Lord, not me or my understanding." ✪

PART III

SPREADING THE FIRE

CHAPTER 12

VALUING THE ANOINTING

In the sixties when I was a young Christian attending the Queensway Cathedral, my pastor Alec Ness said to me, "If you are serious about going into the ministry, watch out for three things: women, money and issues of power and control." That was such helpful advice.

Others have called these snares "the girls, the gold and the glory." How many times have we seen anointed people of God fall because they have succumbed to one of these temptations? The fall is often great, and in full view of all, bringing reproach and much pain on the body of Christ.

This anointed renewal is a holy and breathtaking gift from God. In order for the Holy Spirit to remain with us, we need to place a great value on His manifest presence. We need to be protective of the Father's blessing, living holy lives and keeping our eyes on Jesus.

SET A HIGH VALUE ON THE ANOINTING

Remember how Elisha wouldn't leave until he received Elijah's mantle of anointing? He kept following Elijah; he was persistent and wouldn't leave Elijah's presence until he got a double portion of Elijah's anointing (2 Kin. 2).

Elisha put a very high value on the anointing, much higher than Samson did. Samson had the anointing handed to him; it was his from birth. He did not know what it was like not to have the anointing. Ultimately he took it for granted, not valuing it like Elisha, who had to press in, be persistent and pursue God to receive it. Therefore, Elisha was a better steward of this precious treasure than Samson was.

When it came time for Elisha to pick an assistant, he picked someone who was very diligent, faithful and hard-working. That young man's name was Gehazi.

Gehazi had seen Elisha do many miracles, such as raise the Shunammite woman's boy from the dead and remove poison from food. Gehazi had seen him provide for a prophet's widow with a miraculous supply of oil (2 Kin. 4). Gehazi had seen many supernatural things because the Holy Spirit was at work in the life of Elisha.

Then testing came Gehazi's way. Would Gehazi attach a high value to God's anointing? Or would he treat it as a light thing?

A TIME OF TESTING

Remember the story of Naaman? This was the time Naaman traveled to Elisha to receive healing for his leprosy.

Elisha told him to bathe seven times in the Jordan river, then he would be healed. Remember, this was a test of faith, humility and obedience for Naaman and when he finally obeyed, the Lord healed him totally.

Now Naaman was a very wealthy general, and he returned to Elisha to offer gifts of thanks, saying:

> Now I know that there is no God in all the world except in Israel. Please accept now a gift from your servant (2 Kin. 5:15).

You see, Naaman knew that Elisha's God was the one true God because the personal and intimate power of the Holy Spirit had touched his life and healed him of his leprosy, which no other power, no other god, could do. So he wanted to make an offering. But Elisha answered:

> "As surely as the Lord lives, whom I serve, I will not accept a thing." And even though Naaman urged him, he refused (v. 16).

Now isn't that interesting for a man of God? Most of us as men of God take up an offering every chance we get, don't we? The kingdom always seems to be so short on funds, and if a rich man comes along and says, "Let me give you several thousands dollars," we are very thankful and take it. Elisha felt led by God to decline. God was testing his heart.

Gehazi also knew what it was like to be short on money. Elisha carried on the training of the young prophets that Elijah had begun, and he had hundreds of young men under him. Gehazi was probably often asked, "How are the finances at the school in Jericho or the one in Bethel?" It must have been an important issue to him that there be enough funds, including enough for his own needs.

If we are not careful when it comes to money, we can lean on our own understanding rather than being dependent upon the person of the Holy Spirit and the anointing of God.

Since Elisha wouldn't accept any gifts, Naaman left, extremely grateful to God for His healing.

> After Naaman had traveled some distance, Gehazi, the servant of Elisha the man of God, said to himself, "My master was too easy on Naaman, this Aramean, by not accepting from him what he brought. As surely as the Lord lives, I will run after him and get something from him."
>
> So Gehazi hurried after Naaman (vv. 19-21).

What was going on in Gehazi's heart? He wanted some money, right? He was tired of being poor. Maybe he was thinking of getting some vineyards and olive groves for himself. He must have figured that Elisha would not find out since Elisha did not always know everything that was going on.

Gehazi had gotten used to the anointing, used to being around the supernatural. He had seen miracles happen; they were no longer astonishing to him. Gehazi decided to take matters into his owns hands instead of honoring the word of the Lord through the prophet. Naaman saw Gehazi running after him, and he got down from his chariot to meet him.

> "Is everything all right?" he asked.
>
> "Everything is all right," Gehazi answered. "My master sent me to say, 'Two young men from the company of the prophets have just come to me from the hill country of Ephraim. Please give them a talent of silver and two sets of clothing'" (vv. 21-22).

A talent of silver was about seventy-five pounds, probably

worth thousands of dollars, and it was only a small part of the present that Naaman had brought. So, to get a portion of it Gehazi lied.

Naaman urged Gehazi to take two talents, which he did, along with two sets of clothing. Naaman's servants carried them until they were almost home, then Gehazi took them, put them away in the house and sent the servants away. He went in to his master Elisha as though nothing had happened.

Can you see how this whole thing played right into his greed — and probably his need? Gehazi's whole future was on the line.

> "Where have you been, Gehazi?" Elisha asked.
>
> "Your servant didn't go anywhere," Gehazi answered.
>
> But Elisha said to him, "Was not my spirit with you when the man got down from his chariot to meet you? Is this the time to take money, or to accept clothes, olive groves, vineyards, flocks, herds, or menservants and maidservants?" (vv. 25-26).

All the things that he desired — flocks, herds, servants — that was not the time for them. That is why Elisha had said no, yet Gehazi fell right into the trap. Look what happened to him.

> "Naaman's leprosy will cling to you and to your descendants forever." Then Gehazi went from Elisha's presence and he was leprous, as white as snow (v. 27).

How tragic! Critics have a valid point when they condemn people who put their own needs for popularity, glory and their own agendas ahead of the preciousness of the anointing. These issues cause many to fall away, and it grieves the heart of God. Gehazi was snared by his greed for money. Is this a trap that would tempt you?

As the Holy Spirit brings renewal, people are joyous and blessed, and often they give very generously. Leaders must not take advantage of them. We need to be good stewards of God's finances and flow together in love, being led by the Spirit in these areas.

TRUE RICHES

When the Holy Spirit imparts His anointing to the body of Christ today, testing will come to see if we are going to value the anointing or not. Are we going to treat Him as true riches and not just as someone we can exploit? Jesus tells us that true riches are the things of God.

> Whoever can be trusted with very little can also be trusted with much, and whoever is dishonest with very little will also be dishonest with much. So if you have not been trustworthy in handling worldly wealth, who will trust you with true riches? And if you have not been trustworthy with someone else's property, who will give you property of your own? (Luke 16:10-12).

Jesus is speaking of the true riches — the things of the Spirit.

> No servant can serve two masters. Either he will hate the one and love the other, or he will be devoted to the one and despise the other. You cannot serve both God and Money (v. 13).

I want to remind you how precious the gift of the Holy Spirit's anointing is that God is offering to you and me today. True riches — that's an understatement.

WILLING TO PLAY, WILLING TO PAY

As we move closer to God, the cost goes higher because the anointing becomes greater. The more we are in love with Jesus, the more we need to be honoring the things of the kingdom of God — the true riches (Luke 16:11).

We are pressing in to God saying, "Lord, increase Your anointing. We thank You that Your Spirit comes in power. Thank You that people go under God's power and shake and fall, yet also fall in love with Jesus. But now empower us with prophecy, empower us with gifts of healing, empower us with intercessory prayers of the Spirit, empower us with evangelism so we can go out and get the job done."

As we are asking Him, He is answering our prayers. But I want you to know that the price goes up. As your relationship with Him gets more and more personal, more and more intimate, you must not only "talk the talk" but also "walk the walk." We all need to remain meek and teachable. In marriage it is important not to take intimacy for granted. Neither can we take for granted the Lord's anointing, treating it casually.

Sometimes Christians seek power as the latest "kick." But they don't allow God to do His full work in them; their lives don't change. People cannot come to these meetings day after day and play in the anointing, then go back home to sin. We may get away with it for a little while, but the day will come when there will be a reckoning with the Lord. That is like playing Russian roulette with your soul.

STAY ACCOUNTABLE AND TEACHABLE

You and I are accountable for the wonderful anointing the Lord is giving us. Now that should be exciting. Don't you want to be faithful with this? Don't you want to be a good steward of the true riches that He is placing in your hands? Let us remain teachable and correctable; let us stay humble and in fellowship with one another. We want to stay bolted down to the deck, not become loose cannons that fire off unpredictably and damage God's kingdom.

If you are not accountable to yourself and others, you are putting yourself at great risk by asking God for more of the anointing. Let me say it again, if you are not accountable, not teachable and not willing to be known heart-to-heart, and yet you are pressing in for more of the anointing, you are putting yourself and the church at great risk.

There are two attitudes that set themselves up against God's anointing — quenching the Spirit through fear and an "anything goes" approach to flowing in the Spirit. Though these two are opposites, either can grieve the Spirit. We must value the anointing so much that we stay moldable in God's hands, not set in our own ways — at either end of the spectrum.

Get into a small group somewhere if you are serious about wanting the Lord to use you. Begin to pray with your friends. Say to them, "If you see things in my life that are not right before God, speak to me as a brother and a friend. Will you bring correction if you think I need it?" Be accountable to one another. As we do that, we will find His yoke is easy and His burden is light. Valuing the anointing is not a hard thing.

Great reproach must have come on Elisha's ministry when Gehazi became a leper. Leprosy in Scripture was often a symbol for sin, and certainly Gehazi did sin.

Our hearts grieve every time we hear of another person falling, much as Elisha must have grieved when he made that pronouncement over Gehazi. I can see him with tears running down his face as he asked, "Gehazi, did my heart not go with you when you ran to meet Naaman?" Gehazi lost his perspective on what was valuable, and he was ruined.

The anointing of the Holy Spirit is given to glorify Jesus and bring in the kingdom of God. In His mercy and His love He comes to fill us with true riches so we can partake in what the world desperately needs — intimacy with God, intimacy with Jesus, the reality of His presence — and then give it away. The prayer in my heart is that you would flow in a powerful anointing of the Holy Spirit and bring incredible glory to Jesus Christ — every place you go, in everything you do and in everything you say.

We dare not use the anointing to gain riches or glory or credibility for ourselves in any way. Let Him use us for one purpose and one purpose only — that Jesus, the Son of God, be honored and glorified through your life and mine.

God has already promised to supply all of our needs according to His riches in glory in Christ Jesus (Phil. 4:19). Let's trust Him with everything and not let the girls, the gold and the glory become a snare to us.

Lord, help us to value the true riches You have put among us, the precious presence of Your Holy Spirit. May we not use it to further our own agendas, may we not market it, advertise it or package it and sell it. We just want to come and do what You want to do in us and through us so that the kingdom of God can spread all over the world. ✪

GO FOR THE KINGDOM

Pastors have come to me and said, "John, God's presence wonderfully broke out in our church, and we had some great meetings for three or four weeks, but then it all stopped. Why do you think that happened? Did we do something wrong?"

For a while I did not know. I would just say, "Come on back, get refilled and take it home again." That is still good advice, but I think I have some answers now to those nagging questions.

We are in our second year of renewal in Toronto (twenty

months at the time of this writing). Do you know when this move of God will end? *It will end when the presence of the Holy Spirit stops coming in this way.*

If we want God to continue moving as He has, and if we want to allow Him to take us further, we must love to see God do things His way and not attempt to steady the ark (1 Chr. 13:9).

STAY HUNGRY FOR MORE OF GOD

We read about Peter, James and John answering the call of Christ in Matthew 4:

> As Jesus was walking beside the Sea of Galilee, he saw two brothers, Simon called Peter and his brother Andrew. They were casting a net into the lake, for they were fisherman. "Come, follow me," Jesus said, "and I will make you fishers of men." At once they left their nets and followed him.
>
> Going on from there, he saw two other brothers, James son of Zebedee and his brother John. They were in a boat with their father Zebedee, preparing their nets. Jesus called them, and immediately they left the boat and their father and followed him (vv. 18-22).

When we read this, we think, "What happened there?" These men had lives, businesses and families. Yet when Jesus showed up and called them, they went just like that. Isn't that amazing? But there is more to this story.

In the Gospel of Luke, we read about a prior encounter Jesus had with these future disciples. Jesus had gotten into one of Simon Peter's boats and asked him to push it a little way from shore. Then He started teaching the people who were there.

After He finished, He told Simon to let down his nets for a catch. Simon protested, saying they'd already been fishing all night, but had caught nothing. Then he relented and responded:

> "But because you say so, I will let down the nets" (5:5).

We could speculate here about Peter's tone of voice. He may have sounded impatient. He was frustrated because he knew a little bit about fishing — more that Jesus did, he probably thought. Nevertheless, he chose to obey, and they caught so many fish that their nets began to break. They had to get help to bring all the fish in.

> When Simon Peter saw this, he fell at Jesus' knees and said, "Go away from me, Lord; I am a sinful man!" For he and all his companions were astonished at the catch of fish they had taken, and so were James and John, the sons of Zebedee, Simon's partners.
> Then Jesus said to Simon, "Don't be afraid" (vv. 8-10).

Why was Simon Peter afraid? Because the power of God showed up, and he got the greatest catch of fish he had ever seen. Peter was astounded by the supernatural power of the Holy Spirit. That is why Peter left his boats and nets when Jesus said, "Come and follow Me." He didn't even try to reason with himself about it because he knew he'd seen the power of God. His family, his business, his partners — everything dimmed in the blazing light of God.

Peter was so impacted by this miracle that he walked away from everything he owned. He was hungry for God. If His touch came upon you, would you be willing to leave all to follow Him?

You and I have been given a wonderful opportunity to partake in something that is beyond our wildest dreams and greatest expectations. God is moving powerfully by the Spirit and offering this anointing to whoever will accept it. Are you so hungry for more of God that you will run with it, forsaking all?

COUNT THE COST, THEN PAY THE PRICE!

> The kingdom of heaven is like treasure hidden in a field. When a man found it, he hid it again, and then in his joy went and sold all he had and bought that field (Matt. 13:44).

A man is out poking around — maybe he bought a treasure map somewhere — and he discovers an incredible treasure in a field. He thinks to himself, "If I liquidate my assets, I could buy the whole field. Then the treasure would be mine." It cost him everything, but he got the riches.

If you want the true riches, it is going to cost you something — probably everything. You must embrace the cross. Your lifestyle will change. Carol and I canceled our morning agendas and gave our mornings to God. We "sold" our mornings, "buying" the treasure of intimacy with Christ. How badly do you want to run with Him in this? Will you go for the kingdom?

Desiree Torrie of Willowdale, Ontario, thought that what she'd heard occurring at our church sounded "a little spooky." But in the spring of 1994, she had a dream about her Aunt Judy (who attends our church) holding a large gold bar, which turned into a very bright white light as Desiree went closer to examine it.

For several months Desiree tried to figure out this dream. She asked others about our church, but people discouraged her from going, saying that they'd never go there. "Since they were much more religious than I, the advice was worth listening to," Desiree says. "However, I was curious."

That July a friend of Desiree's wanted to visit our church, so they arrived together, "very intentionally with no pen to sign our names to anything." Desiree didn't want to pay the price of risking, of laying down her reputation. But she pressed through that. She marveled at the people she saw worshiping: "The nations were there. The young, the old, the rich, the poor, the learned, the uneducated. It did not take long for me to realize that this was real. There was no superstar, there was no hocus-pocus."

She allowed her Aunt Judy and a pastor to pray for her, and he told her to forgive the person who rear-ended her in an automobile accident several years ago. She explains:

As soon as I heard the word *forgive*, I fell to the ground and entered into a two-and-a-half hour exchange with God. As I began to forgive others, I was being forgiven. Brought into my mind for forgiveness was everyone, including my childhood friend who at five years of age broke my china tea set.

A man from the ministry team praying over her announced what he was seeing: "It's beautiful. It's a very tight flower bud which is beginning to blossom." Desiree confesses, "The vision was correct. My Christian walk had always been a bud. I just never knew that it could blossom."

Several months later, Desiree reported that God had given her opportunities to witness to and intercede for several people, six of whom gave their lives to Jesus — including her husband.

Desiree counted the cost and took the risk. Her lifestyle changed; it blossomed. She walks in joy and freedom, using every opportunity to tell others about Jesus, but it cost her something — her old lifestyle.

Desiree found the treasure and bought the field. She is joyfully living for God.

STEP OUT IN HIS STRENGTH

God doesn't want saying, "We did this ourselves, we prayed this down. We organized ourselves and strategized for this and brought in the best of speakers. Aren't we great?" The Lord wants to be able to say, "I took the least among you and did the greatest work."

> The Lord said to Gideon, "You have too many men for me to deliver Midian into their hands. In order that Israel may not boast against me that her own strength has saved her, announce now to the people, 'Anyone who trembles with fear may turn back and leave Mount Gilead.'" So twenty-two thousand men left, while ten thousand remained (Judg. 7:2-3).

God eventually pared this army of Gideon's down to three hundred men. He wanted everyone to know this victory was from Him, not by the strength of human resources.

This renewal is not going to work with the arm of flesh — with strategies and programs. Nor will it work if people let fear slow them down as they try to keep it tidy. The Spirit of God today is coming in power, and it is going to become greater, much greater. And it is His sovereign work. We need to step out in faith and continue calling on Him as He leads and directs.

Reverend Les Barker and his wife, Bonnie, of St. Ninian's Anglican Church in Scarborough, Ontario, have been coming to our services regularly and serve on the ministry team. In November 1994, they visited with clergy friends at St. Luke's Episcopal Church in Akron, Ohio. Their friends unexpectedly invited Les and Bonnie to give their testimony about this renewal. Then they prayed for people. Les describes what happened:

> During prayer ministry about 15 percent of the congregation came for "more." It was so exciting...most were drinking deeply and being filled with the love of God. One young woman remained on the floor "receiving" for about an hour. When she got up she said to me, with sparkling eyes and tear-streaked face, "He is real! He is still holding my hand."
>
> Bonnie and I feel so humbled, privileged and excited about being used by God to light this fire.

Les and Bonnie stepped out in God's strength and He was there to meet them.

When the manifest presence of God is among us like this, it is the time to rise up and run. Do not run if God is not among you. But when God is among you, run with everything that is within you — run, run, run, run!

The Holy Spirit is saying, "Is it not enough for you to have Me powerfully in your midst? Is it not enough for you to have the mighty presence of the Lord? Does that not so encourage you, give you boldness and favor, to enable you to go for the kingdom as never before?"

We've got to go for the kingdom of God wholeheartedly. We are going to sell out and buy the field because we want the treasure. We want Jesus. We want the power of God and the kingdom of God to come, and we are going to surrender to Him and the things He wants to do.

This is a call to run with the Holy Spirit who is upon us. Are you going to lean on His strength and go for it with everything that is within you?

ASK GOD FOR ANSWERS, THEN RUN WITH THEM

To tell you the truth, when the Lord began to pour this out I was afraid that I might somehow offend the Holy Spirit and His presence would not come anymore. I asked, "Lord, what do I do?" He gave me one word: "Ask." Before we go charging ahead taking things into our own hands, we must remember to ask, "Lord, is this You? Should we go ahead with this?" And if He gives us the OK, run with it. That was David's heart.

> Once more the Philistines came up and spread out in the Valley of Rephaim; so David inquired of the Lord, and he answered, "Do not go straight up, but circle around behind them and attack them in front of the balsam trees. As soon as you hear the sound of marching in the tops of the balsam trees, move quickly, because that will mean the Lord has gone out in front of you to strike the Philistine army." So David did as the Lord commanded him, and he struck down the Philistines all the way from Gibeon to Gezer (2 Sam. 5:22-25).

David asked God what to do, then he ran with what God told him. He had the confidence to do that because he knew that God had gone out ahead of him.

I can hear the sound of the marching in the treetops. A supernatural, heavenly army is present in our meetings, going out ahead of us. If we ask and obey God, we will be led by God, by His army marching ahead to lead the way.

I hear the supernatural sound of the army of the Lord in my spirit — the internal sensing and awareness of His purposes. God said, "When you hear that, run for it with everything that is within you because God has gone out ahead of you."

Are you ready to run? Or are you going to play it safe and

say, "I know the kind of problems that will come up. I had better be careful." Listen, when you hear the sound of marching in the top of the balsam trees when you sense that the Sovereign Lord is with you, then it's the time to run, because if you do, the victory will be yours.

GO FOR THE KINGDOM!

The nation of Israel had just come out of Egypt by the powerful hand of God. No one amongst them should have had any doubt about God's provision and protection. They had watched the Egyptian army who pursued them disappear in the waters of the Red Sea. Now God led them through the desert with a cloud by day and a pillar of fire by night. They were fed morning and evening by His supernatural hand.

When they arrived at the land God had promised them, twelve men were sent to spy it out for forty days. When they returned, they brought back a wonderful report on how fruitful and productive the land was. But they were afraid of its powerful inhabitants and its fortified cities. Caleb, however, knew that with God they were more than able to conquer. He alone had the eyes to see and the ears to hear that God was with them, and they were invincible.

> Then Caleb silenced the people before Moses and said, "We should go up and take possession of the land, for we can certainly do it."
>
> But the men who had gone up with him said, "We can't attack those people; they are stronger than we are." And they spread among the Israelites a bad report about the land they have explored. They said, "The land we explored devours those living it. All the people we saw there are of great size. We saw the Nephilim [giants] there (the descendants of Anak come from the Nephilim). We

seemed like grasshoppers in our own eyes, and we looked the same to them" (Num. 13:30-33).

So the nation of Israel missed their great opportunity to possess the kingdom of God. Because of fear and unbelief, the Lord told them that they would spend the next forty years in the wilderness — one year for each of the forty days they spent exploring the land (14:34). How tragic!

God came along with a once-in-a-lifetime opportunity, and few saw it. Why did only Joshua and Caleb trust God fully and want to do great exploits in His name? What was the matter with the rest of them? Couldn't everyone see the cloud, the pillar of fire? Didn't they remember the Red Sea and the waters of Meribah that were healed? Did they not eat the manna every morning? *God was with them!*

Caleb's heart said, "If God be for us, who can be against us? Let us go and get them. They will be bread for us. We will eat those men alive."

But everybody else was saying, "Now let us not get carried away here; let us use a little wisdom." They looked at the circumstances and quickly forgot how big and capable God really is.

Right now God is giving you and me an opportunity to participate in the greatest revival opportunity I have ever seen in over forty years as a Christian. Let's go for it with everything that is within us. Yes, there are problems; yes, there is the flesh; yes, we miss it sometimes. But the power of God is being poured out here and around the world. Let's not miss this opportunity to be a part of what God is doing.

Jesus wept over the city of Jerusalem.

O Jerusalem, Jerusalem, you who kill the prophets and stone those sent to you, how often I have longed to gather your children together, as a hen gathers her chicks under her wings, but you were not willing. Look, your house is left you to desolate (Matt. 23:37-38).

They did not know the hour of their visitation from God. They didn't recognize the time when He was among them.

Bill and Melinda Fish, pastors of the Church of the Risen Saviour in Trafford, Pennsylvania, wrote to tell Carol and me about Melinda's last experience in our services here in Toronto. God touched "a dry place" in her heart, and she laughed, wept and cried out over and over, "This is the day of visitation! It was as though the Lord was having a good time making me say it like a teacher would make a mischievous student write it on a chalkboard a thousand times!"

Do you know what is happening in Toronto and around the world? This is the day of visitation! The Holy Spirit of God is actually coming and touching people. As long as we welcome Him, as long as we love His ways, as long as we honor Him, as long as we're not embarrassed by Him, as long as we are radical enough to go for it and not play it safe, *He will keep coming*. But He is looking for a people who are full of boldness, people who will leave their boats and nets and follow Jesus; people who will buy the field, who will enter the promised land. Will you risk your resources and reputation, and become one of these?

The Cost
of the Party

W hen all of this began, I had no desire for Christians to fall down, roll around and laugh. I had seen people do that before. I was asking God for His power to come, and save the lost, heal the sick and expand the kingdom.

That's the direction I wanted to see God move. It never occurred to me that the Spirit of God desired to bring a tremendous wave of joy to flood over His people so they would laugh and get excited and enjoy His presence. Therefore, when all of this started happening, I was startled because those being powerfully touched were all our church people. I knew them. I knew that they wouldn't fake this! They were solid in their faith, and many of them were able ministers in the Spirit themselves.

So it took me a little while to say, "This is very good." It took me a while to be grateful because it was not what I was expecting or praying for.

Then, as we discovered the biblical and historical basis for what God was doing, we realized God was doing a special work of renewal and said, "OK, Lord, if You just want to love up on us, then we will enjoy what You are doing right now."

Now I see that it is vital for the church to fall deeply in love with Jesus again. When you are really in love, you may act a little bit crazy, but nothing seems too great, nothing seems insurmountable. I believe we need to be restored to that place. That is what Jesus is calling us back to — our first love.

AN ABUNDANCE OF NEW WINE

To understand the joy and the "party" we are experiencing now, let's see what happened at another party — a wedding that Jesus attended.

The host ran out of wine early, and Jesus' mother told Him about it. Then she instructed the servants to do whatever Jesus told them. That is really good advice.

> Nearby stood six stone water jars, the kind used by the Jews for ceremonial washing, each holding from twenty to thirty gallons.
>
> Jesus said to the servants "Fill the jars with water"; they filled them to the brim.
>
> Then he told them, "Now draw some out and take it to the master of the banquet." They did so, and the master of the banquet tasted the water

207

that had been turned into wine. He did not realize where it had come from, though the servants who had drawn the water knew.

Then he called the bridegroom aside and said, "Everyone brings out the choice wine first and then the cheaper wine after the guests have had too much to drink; but you have saved the best till now." This, the first of his miraculous signs, Jesus performed in Cana of Galilee. He thus revealed his glory (John 2:6-11).

His miracles still reveal His glory. Jesus has saved the best till last. New wine is being poured out in the body of Christ in these last days, and it is the best we have ever tasted. It is so full of joy, so full of power, so full of life. It is fabulously fantastic. It is also very contagious.

People come here from England or Australia or Japan and have a party for three or four nights and get drunk and overcome in the Holy Spirit. Then they take it home and start pouring it out to their friends. Isn't that amazing? Yet it happens, time and time again.

Why were those water jars filled to the brim? So there would be plenty for all. Jesus had the servants set aside 150 gallons of water that had the potential to become wine. They simply had to dip and pour. They could have partied all week on that amount of wine. There is an abundant supply with the Lord Jesus, an abundant supply.

Many people hang back and say, "Let someone else have the prayer. There are other people who need it more than I do."

An Anglican minister's wife came to our Catch the Fire conference in October 1994, tired and resentful at how busy they were. She knew she was not seeking the Lord's face; she let her husband do all the "spiritual stuff." She said she was good at observing and would spend most of her time watching and not receiving. However, that changed when she came to Toronto. This is how she described what happened to her at our conference:

> Over these past four days I have been on the carpet...I feel I have been revived, gently corrected and empowered. I have had prophecy prayed over me. I've seen it happen to others, but now I've submitted to His hand and will for my life.
> P.S. Before I was a Christian, I drank a lot. My dad is an alcoholic. I feel God has allowed me to drink the new wine and be drunk in Him. Oh, it's so much better than the old wine!

Listen, God has provided an abundant supply; we have tapped into the ocean here. Here is all the new wine and the new life you will ever need. You do not have to conserve it. You do not have to be careful. There is even wine to waste. All you have to do is dip your jug in, pour it out, and — wow — it's wine.

How many of us have dipped in for years and every time we pulled out the jug it was just water? Carol and I are doing all the same things we had been doing for years, but when we started pouring it out in January 1994, suddenly it was wine. It shocked us, really. It took quite a while to get accustomed to it; in fact, we are still not used to it. I can hardly grasp it now. All I know is, He has saved the best till last, and there is an abundance for the thirsty.

JESUS PICKED UP THE TAB

Not everybody likes what we do here. Some think we are crazy and do not want any part of this. I believe they are missing out on a tremendous blessing of God. People are having a wonderful time in the presence of the Lord. The changes and fruit that results are brilliant testimony to the glory of God, but would God throw a party?

I did not have a theological framework for "parties" when this started. I had to relearn facts like, the angels rejoice and "party" every time one sinner repents and comes into the kingdom of God. Just think, there are thousands of them every day, so it must be a continual party in heaven.

But parties are expensive. We do well to ask, "Who is paying for this? Who is picking up the tab?" Jesus has paid for it all.

> They came to place called Golgotha (which means The Place of the Skull). There they offered Jesus wine to drink, mixed with gall; but after tasting it, he refused to drink it. When they had crucified him, they divided up his clothes by casting lots. And sitting down, they kept watch over him there. Above his head they placed the written charge against him: This is Jesus, the King of the Jews (Matt. 27:33-37).

They crucified the One who had never done anything wrong in His whole life. He raised the widow's dead son; He healed the woman with an issue of blood; He raised the dead daughter of the religious leader; He healed the servant of the Roman centurion. Everywhere He went He gave life and blessing and peace and joy. It was the greatest party that country had ever seen.

But they took this precious Lamb of God and stretched out His hands and nailed them to the cross with huge Roman spikes. Then they drove another one through those precious feet and put a mocking sign over His head, "This is Jesus, the King of the Jews." They stripped Him and hoisted Him up between heaven and earth. There, at a busy intersection, naked and in tremendous agony, bleeding from His head, His back, His hands, His feet, hung the precious Son of God. Why? For you and for me.

This is the cost of the party. He was nailed to the cross, the most hideous instrument of torture ever devised by the demented minds of men. He had to pull Himself up, working those wounds afresh in His feet and hands, just to take another breath. Six hours of this — naked, humiliated — all for you and me.

This is what they said of Him:

> Two robbers were crucified with him, one on his right and one on his left. Those who passed by hurled insults at him, shaking their heads and saying, "You who are going to destroy the temple and build it in three days, save yourself! Come down from the cross, if you are the Son of God!"
>
> In the same way the chief priests, the teachers of the law and the elders mocked him. "He saved others," they said, "but he can't save himself! He's the king of Israel! Let him come down now from the cross, and we will believe in him. He trusts in God. Let God rescue him now if he wants him, for he said, 'I am the Son of God.'"
>
> In the same way the robbers who were crucified with him also heaped insults on him (Matt. 27:38-44).

He was utterly rejected by men. In His most helpless, vulnerable hour, He was mocked and insulted.

> From the sixth hour until the ninth hour darkness came over all the land. About the ninth hour Jesus cried out in a loud voice, *"Eloi, Eloi, lama sabachthani?"* — which means, "My God, my God, why have you forsaken me?"
>
> When some of those standing there heard this, they said, "He's calling Elijah." Immediately one of them ran and got a sponge. He filled it with wine

211

vinegar, put it on a stick, and offered it to Jesus to drink. But the rest said, "Leave him alone. Let's see if Elijah comes to save him."

And when Jesus had cried out again in a loud voice, he gave up his spirit (vv. 45-50).

He hung up on that cross, and that precious blood from that perfect life poured out and dripped down to the foot of that cross. When His life blood was all but drained out, the Father came with your sins and mine and placed them upon that broken body that was marred more than any man. Then the Father quickly turned away.

Jesus could have come down from the cross. He could have called the angels to free Him. It was love that held Him there, not the nails. He knew that He was to offer His perfect, sinless life as a ransom, an exchange for our guilty sinful lives. That would satisfy God's justice and provide a basis for God's mercy and forgiveness. When you and I are enjoying this wonderful "party" and release of joy, may we be ever mindful of the cost.

HIS BLOOD CLEANSES US

Years ago I talked with God about the cross. "Father, I know You love Jesus so much. Why then did You allow such an agonizing death for Him?" I reasoned that John the Baptist was beheaded, which was quick. So were the deaths of many of the saints. "Why did Jesus have to suffer so much?"

The Father showed me something very precious. During His crucifixion, I believe Jesus actually bled to death. All those hours on the cross, His precious blood flowed from those fresh wounds until the moment arrived when He was about to pass out from the loss of blood. At that moment, the Father took the sins of the world and placed them upon that broken, emaciated body, and Jesus became sin who knew no sin.

God made him who had no sin to be sin for us, so
that in him we might become the righteousness of
God (2 Cor. 5:21).

The Father, who could not look upon such horror, turned
away, and Jesus cried out in the midst of that terrible sepa-
ration, "My God, My God, why have you forsaken me?"
(Matt. 27:46). It was the first time in all eternity that their
intimate fellowship was broken. What a tremendous price
to pay. (Read Isaiah 53 to begin to understand Jesus' agony
over carrying the sin of the world.)

Yet we need to see something else. He had been bleeding profusely for six hours. His blood had already been
poured out before the sins of the world were placed upon
Him. That holy blood was never contaminated by the sins
of the world. His blood remains holy, untouched by your
sins and mine. It is as pure and holy as ever, full of mercy
and life. It was *His body* that was broken and contaminated.

That is why the book of Hebrews says the blood of Jesus
cries better things than the blood of Abel (12:24). The blood
of Abel was crying out for revenge: "God, do something.
My brother has murdered me." But what does the blood of
Jesus cry? "Father, forgive them for they know not what
they do. For these guilty people, Lord, I will provide the
way to mercy. I will take their place. Let mercy be given
them." In essence He said, "I am trading My life for theirs."

When we are having the party of a lifetime, as we have
been for all these months, we need to remember who is
picking up the tab. It is Jesus, our glorious King. There is
not another king like Him on the face of the earth or in all
of heaven. Kings have come and gone, but not one of them
has loved his people enough to die for them.

But death could not hold Him. Power entered that tomb,
and He was raised from the dead with the same power that
is filling us today, the precious Holy Spirit. Life came into

that body, and He was resurrected. He lives today; He lives forever, making intercession for you and me.

Jesus gave Himself so you and I could enjoy the glory and the joy, the blessing and peace of heaven and all that it holds. He delights to come and win your heart. Isn't He wonderful? Isn't He precious? King of kings and Lord of lords. He has restored us into a living, loving and vital relationship with the Father.

FROM DEATH TO LIFE

It may be that you have never been born again. You need to give your life to Jesus Christ and make Him Lord. He did not die just for the world; he died for you. He is offering to become your personal Savior, and He will take your place at the judgment of God if you ask Him, allowing you to free.

Or you may have known Jesus at one time, but something has destroyed that relationship. Perhaps you got careless or you were offended by something. You said, "If that is Christianity, you can keep it." You walked away from the Lord of life, got mad at God and decided to punish Him by sinning. Don't play into the enemy's hands; he just wants to destroy you. Jesus came that you might have life and have it more abundantly (John 10:10).

The good news of the gospel is that you can be completely forgiven, completely welcomed into the family of God, into the kingdom of love, by a free gift of grace. You can have eternal life by faith.

Admit that you're guilty. Tell Him you're sorry for hurting Him and others. Ask Him for His mercy.

You may feel the Holy Spirit drawing you and tugging at your heart right now saying, "You need to give your life to Jesus Christ. You need to have your sins forgiven and have Jesus rescue you from the certain judgment of God." If this describes your situation, please pray these words out loud right now:

Dear heavenly Father, I know that I have sinned. I know that I have done many things wrong in my life. There have been occult sins, sexual sins and violent sins. I have sinned greatly against You and against others. I owe You a great debt, and I have nothing to repay You with. I need Jesus, Your resurrected Son, our Savior, to pay it for me. I know He died so I may live. Come into my heart and life, Lord Jesus. I want You to be my King and Lord forever.

God's Word defines why we are to pray this out loud.

That if you confess with your mouth, "Jesus is Lord," and believe in your heart that God raised him from the dead, you will be saved. For it is with your heart that you believe and are justified, and it is with your mouth that you confess and are saved (Romans 10:9-10).

You will be saved. The Bible clearly says in John 3:16:

For God so loved the world that he gave his one and only Son, that whoever believes in him shall not perish but have eternal life.

That is why the gospel is such good news. Christ's work is a finished work. There's nothing for you to do but believe. I'm not saying, "Get yourself together, become perfect, then come and see if God will accept you." No, He takes you just as you are and gives you the gift of eternal life based on what Jesus has already done for you.

You have just passed from death to life if you prayed that prayer and meant it in your heart. You have gone from nothing to everything. If you know Jesus, your life is already a success. ❂

CHAPTER 15

SPREADING THE FIRE

It's now exciting to go to church!" That's what the letter said that I received from a man who visited the Airport Vineyard with his wife. "Well," you may say, "that's nice. What's the big deal?" Well, the big deal is that he's the pastor!

When Pastor Charles Babcock and his wife were in Toronto, they had no "startling manifestations," although he reported that he felt overwhelmed with God's love for him. On the airplane ride home, however, they both questioned whether they had anything to take back to their church,

Bouquet Baptist Church in Santa Clarita, California.

On the first Sunday back they shared about their trip and asked if anyone wanted prayer for refreshing. Pastor Babcock relates what happened:

> Ninety percent of the church came forward, and we spent the next hour praying for them. Immediately God began to set some free from terrible childhood experiences and heal the memories of their pain...Much to my delight, the first person God dealt with in that way was our worship leader. He's a totally new man, and our worship has taken a dramatic turn for the better.

This pastor's story is repeated many times, the world over.

THE WORLD OVER

After God showed Himself powerfully in our services, the word spread, and people started coming. After a couple of months, we had people attending our services from all over the world.

Our average attendance in 1994 was about one thousand people a night and in 1995 fifteen hundred people per night. In any given meeting one-third will indicate they are first-time attendees. A total attendance of over 750,000 people have come to our meeting to date. Every meeting we ask all those who are pastors or church leaders to stand, and the average is about 10 percent of the people present. We estimate that twenty-five thousand different pastors and leaders have visited.

These people have taken the Father's blessing back to their countries. For instance, this renewal has spread rapidly in England. Eleanor Mumford, the wife of John Mumford, senior pastor of the Southwest London Vineyard, came to our church in April 1994. On returning home she told of her experience in Holy Trinity Brompton (Church of England) in London, and the renewal broke out there and continued spreading throughout England.

I was thrilled when Gerald Coates, leader of the Pioneer Churches in Britain, told me that there are five to seven thousand churches in the U.K. now that are flowing in the Spirit's power (there are forty-nine thousand churches total). If there are only ten people in each church on the ministry team praying, including the pastor, that means there are at least fifty thousand people in Britain beginning in a new way to do the works that Jesus did. That is exciting. Oh Lord, bring us more, bring more, bring more!

The church in Great Britain has undergone tremendous change in the last fifteen years, which has contributed to this renewal in a remarkable way. The house church movement, John Wimber's influence, the March for Jesus event, Spring Harvest events with thousands participating, the Alpha courses — all of these are part of the changes in the body of Christ in Britain.

Perhaps most important are the incredible efforts toward church unity by Clive Calver of the Evangelical Alliance and by Gerald Coates of the Pioneer movement. These efforts have brought most of the nation's church leaders into fellowship and working relationships, so the church was strongly networked and ready for renewal to come.

This renewal is strong not only in Britain but now in Germany, Switzerland, the Netherlands, Scandinavia, South Africa, New Zealand, Australia, Thailand, Korea, Indonesia and even Japan. Some of the hot spots in North America are Pasadena, California; Seattle, Washington; Dallas, Texas; Melbourne, Florida and New England. In Canada renewal has broken out strongly in Victoria, B.C., Ottawa, Ontario, and on the east coast in St. Johns, N.B. We believe this is just the beginning.

Many countries are experiencing a move of the Holy Spirit totally independent of us, such as Argentina (which has been in its own orbit for several years), India and China. But the same themes prevail — falling in love with Jesus again, unity of all believers, a hunger for more of God and a new enthusiasm for bringing in the lost.

The Holy Spirit is not limited. He can be with us here in Canada and also be in Britain, in Australia and everywhere else — all at the same time. This refreshing of God is being multiplied over the whole earth. The works of Jesus Christ and works of the kingdom of God are rapidly going ahead right before our eyes. What glorious days we live in! I can barely grasp the current impact of it all, let alone the future implications.

SPREADING THE FIRE THROUGH PASTORS

During the outpouring of the Holy Spirit at Azusa Street, many people were freshly touched and empowered. Nevertheless, Azusa Street is not particularly known for all the conversions that took place there. It is known for pastors and leaders who were powerfully touched by the Holy Spirit who then took the blessing home to their churches and started revivals locally. That is where the harvest came from. Azusa lasted only three years, and yet that revival is still going on. The Pentecostal movement started in April 1906, and according to Vinson Synan, now there are 460 million Pentecostal/charismatics worldwide — 25 percent of all Christians.[1]

We have a thick file with faxes and letters of appreciation from pastors and leaders testifying that God has transformed their lives and ministries. The fruit that we have seen is so wondrous, so healing and so life-giving. We are astounded. Pastors and leaders are coming from the United States, Britain, Europe or elsewhere overseas, not to be saved, but to catch the fire and take it home. The

219

anointing is being carried around the world.

For Carol and me personally, this has been the greatest blessing of all. We believe this is a church-based, pastor-led renewal. It is of the utmost importance that this move of God is led by "ordinary" pastors in a local setting. We need thousands of them, rather than ten, twenty or even one hundred well-known evangelists who only come though areas occasionally. We need pastors who are on the job daily, moving under a powerful anointing of the Holy Spirit, and they need to train their people to do the same. It will take all the leaders and every church and even then:

> The harvest is plentiful but the workers are few.
> Ask the Lord of the harvest, therefore, to send out
> workers into his harvest field (Matt. 9:37-38).

Oh, Lord, give us an army of workers who move in the power and anointing of God! Too many times pastors have been left out of the "loop" of the newest blessing to go through their church. They need to be the first to know. But the word is out now. Tens of thousands of pastors are attending meetings like ours around the world, and they are "catching the fire." They often come cautiously to see for themselves, then end up receiving the greatest blessing of their lives.

We had an Anglican pastor here who said, "I was so down that I was seriously contemplating taking my own life." That is how desperate some men of God are. They are so discouraged by trying to work the program, keep the traditions of the church and make everybody happy. There is no life or love in that. He got filled with God, and when he got up off the floor, everything was changed. He was in love with Jesus and ready to go home and impact his city for the Lord. That is good fruit.

Carol and I are not particularly interested in holding large crusades all over the world to see if we can pack out a stadium somewhere. Our main focus when we travel is to be with pastors and nurture this in churches which have already caught the fire. We want to encourage this new move in local churches. Only the church of Jesus Christ worldwide is large enough to contain what God is wanting to do, and He wants to use all of us.

GOOD REPORTS OF THE FIRE SPREADING

A great many ministries, denominations and churches have been impacted at some level through what God has been doing here at the Airport Vineyard. In addition, many other churches have had an outpouring of the Spirit quite independently of anything we have done. God is going forth with a vengeance to bring His kingdom to the planet. As quoted before:

> The Lord will march out like a mighty man; like a
> warrior he will stir up his zeal with a shout.
> He will raise the battle cry and will triumph over
> his enemies.
>
> For a long time I have kept silent, I have been
> quiet and held myself back.
> But now like a woman in childbirth, I cry out, I
> gasp and I pant (Is. 42:13-14).

God is on the move today! The City Church in Bellevue, Washington, reports that they have "enthusiastically embraced the renewing movement of the Holy Spirit." They have seen miracles, marriages being restored, prodigal children returning to God, emotional and physical healings and regular salvations. "God is accomplishing in minutes by His Holy Spirit what would have taken us decades, if ever, to accomplish in our own strength."

Gerry Plunkett and his wife, Marcia, pastors of Église

Chrétienne de l'Ouest in Pierrefonds, Québec, faxed me that things have changed since they attended services at our church. Gerry says, "I love Jesus as never before. Our prayer life has changed, our married life has changed, our relationship with our children has changed, and boy! has church ever changed! A lot of carpet time and a lot of transformed hearts!"

Gerry tells me about a woman, Linda Girard, whose father had been brutally murdered in August 1994 for the "fun" of it. The Sunday after Gerry and Marcia attended our Catch the Fire conference in October 1994, they prayed for this woman, and she fell backward and was trembling on the floor for an hour and a half. She told them that during that time the Lord showed her a briefcase full of all her negative feelings about the murder. He went through every file with her, one by one.

A month later she testified to the congregation that she was set free and held no animosity against her father's killer. Gerry was impressed to pray for her again, and she went down again, this time for two and a half hours. The next Sunday she reported that the Lord poured His love into her heart for the man who killed her father. She is going to forgive him in person as soon as the Lord directs.

Bill and Melinda Fish, pastors of the Church of the Risen Saviour in Trafford, Pennsylvania, wrote that their church has "begun to revive from the dead." People don't want to miss a service — they want to see what God will do. They have begun renewal weekends once a month to spread this renewal to others in the Pittsburgh area. "There is such an excitement and hunger for God that it is to the point that people who were on the verge of giving up are hungry for the Lord."

From the Czech Republic and missionary organization ACET Czech Republic, we heard the account of a man named Peter who was saved in a tent meeting the previous summer. They prayed for him, and he "stood in a trancelike state for about one hour." When the meeting was finished, with people chatting around him, he suddenly crashed to the ground. Later he got up "quite happily, with a beatific grin on his face." Missionary Stuart Angus adds, "Peter is a salesman for Coca-Cola. He's finally found the real thing!"

Stuart tells us that in a week-long youth festival in which 350 Czech youth attended, the Holy Spirit "swept the meetings, with people experiencing laughter, crying, shaking and falling down." Stuart relates that the meetings lasted from 7:00 P.M. until 3:00 A.M., and the youth still wanted more and more! "Non-believers attending the festival were converted and great enthusiasm was present."

Reverend H. Petrus Nawawi from West Java, Indonesia, wrote to tell me that after their visit to our church in Toronto in January 1995 their whole congregation experienced "the same thing." On his first Sunday back, he shared about their visit here, and the Holy Spirit came in a mighty way, with people laughing, falling down and weeping. He decided not to preach his sermon but ask for more anointing. They canceled their regular services and held renewal meetings all week.

A week later during a meeting of twenty-eight leaders from all over Indonesia, they waited on the Lord. All the leaders experienced renewal; some were unable to speak; some were drunk in the Spirit. According to Rev. Nawawi, this has now spread "all over Indonesia."

Pastor John Overholt of Willow Point Foursquare Gospel Church in Campbell River, B.C., reports:

> I've never experienced such a oneness coming into the body of Christ — and what keeps amazing me is that it's not letting up. We've had *our* attempts at revival meetings in the past, but nothing like what's been happening here. A group of

us pastors has been meeting for prayer once a week for the past four years, but since May [1994], it's like we've been knit together. Getting together before was a good thing, but since this renewal we're actually getting together because we like each other, and we like being around each other. Local church competitiveness has gone way down, and we are truly working together more as it says in Mark 8:35: "for my [Christ's] sake and the gospel's."

Ken and Lois Gott came to Toronto in August 1994 and were thoroughly "blasted." They went home to their Assembly of God church in Sunderland, England, and have had continuous nightly meetings ever since. God is profoundly impacting their city with many conversions and much blessing.

Terry Moore, pastor of Sojourn Church in Dallas, Texas, and members of his staff came to our church in March 1994 after hearing amazing reports about what was happening here. Although Terry relates that he did not have any unusual manifestations, he and his staff all experienced a refreshing of the Holy Spirit. They felt a much greater revelation of the Father's love and a greater sense of the presence of the Lord than ever before. They were deeply stirred to grow in intimacy with God.

Upon returning to Dallas, they shared their experiences with their church. Terry asked for those who wanted to be blessed to come forward, and people literally ran to the front to receive prayer. The Holy Spirit empowered them, and they ministered for hours.

They met every night for the following few weeks and eventually to one meeting a week. People experienced miracles, healings, inner healings and deliverances; they received the joy of the Lord, the peace of God and His wonderful love. Terry and a team from his church traveled to Vietnam and Cambodia that fall. Everywhere they went the same things happened. People received the Holy Spirit in the same manner as he saw in Toronto. In May 1995, Terry and his wife traveled to Switzerland, Romania and Spain. He relates:

> Again the Holy Spirit was poured out. What an unbelievable experience to see God move in people's lives even when we could not speak their languages. These trips just reinforced to me what God is doing and wanting to do in a much greater way.
>
> "The Toronto blessing" has increased our awareness of the work of the Holy Spirit in us and through us. We will never be the same. It is so much fun to be used to touch people, knowing that it is not you but the Holy Spirit who is wanting to love His people in a real and intimate way.

EVANGELISM AS A FRUIT OF THIS RENEWAL

As Carol related when talking about her vision, this renewal seems to be the beginning of a large outpouring. The final phase, so to speak, will be gathering in the lost. We are already seeing some of this happening, though not in the numbers we expect to see later.

In our church we have seen about five thousand people respond to the invitation to commit or recommit their lives to Christ since this move started (January 1994 to September 1995). About 20 percent of those were first-time commitments — people being born again. In terms of the amount of people who have come through here, (250,000 different individuals) that is not a lot. Still, it represents many more than we ever had previously. In fact, we saw more commitments in the first two or three months than we had in our entire previous fifteen years of pastoral ministry.

Evangelism, though, is also being done on a one-to-one level by people who are overflowing with God's blessing and by people who have a new love for the lost.

Regina Frohms came to Toronto from her home in Germany and returned with a deep love for God in her heart. On her next trip here for a conference, she told us what else God did. Regina received a compassion for the lost. In one meeting she cried for a couple of hours for those outside God's kingdom.

A few weeks after Regina returned home, she went with her daughter on a King's Kids missions trip. Her twelve-year-old daughter told her, "Mommy, at first I thought you were crazy." Then her daughter began to cry. She was on the floor for almost an hour, crying. When she got up, she said, "I can understand now what Jesus felt for the lost." Regina told us through tears:

> It was the greatest joy for me to see my children take this love. We had an experience that same day where we led a young drug addict to the Lord on the street together. It was so amazing for me. It's my deepest desire to keep this love for Him and bring it to the lost.

I am surprised when people who are not even saved come to one of our meetings, but it happens. A committed Christian woman from London, England, who was on the ministry team of her church came to our meetings. Her unsaved husband said, "I do not like the idea of you going to Canada alone. I will go with you." She never could get him to go to church in England. He was a very nice man, but he was not Christian.

Well, he came to the first meeting because he wanted to see what she was involved with, and the Lord hooked him. He came every night, and about the third night, he gave his heart to Christ. Of course, that was the highlight for her.

Many people have told us that they can't help telling people about the Lord after being here. Sometimes the manifestations continue after they leave our meetings. Eighteen-year-old Shawna Hull wrote me that she continued to have trouble standing and made weird noises — "at the mall, the restaurant, on the phone, even at school." She added, "I'll tell you one thing, when that starts happening to you in public, God comes into a conversation quite quickly."

David and Lin Saunders, pastors of the Anglican Church in Cullompton, England, became involved in ministry at Exeter Prison after receiving a vision at our church. They are now seeing "hardened criminals coming to Christ — amongst others, murderers, kidnappers, rapists and drug smugglers." What seemed impossible and took years to accomplish is now taking place in an hour. While these men are out in the Spirit on the floor, God is working in them. Many of the men fall on their faces, often with tears of repentance. David and Lin say, "Many of these converted prisoners are maturing quickly and becoming effective workers for Jesus, often with pastoral oversight of other prisoners."

Ché Ahn is now having renewal meetings five nights a week in Pasadena. Youth pastor Scott Ross of the Monrovia Vineyard brought his youth group to a meeting and said none of them really got touched. But the two non-Christians they brought with them fell on the ground under the power of the Holy Spirit. When they got up they said, "We want to give our lives to Jesus Christ."

If the Lord can get His presence into our hearts so we become filled with His love, we will then start to give it away and bless one another. Then the love and life of God will flow. When this happens we will see multitudes of lost souls coming into God's kingdom. Remember, it is a kingdom of love!

WHAT'S NEXT?

Mahesh Chavda and his wife came to our meetings in January 1995. Mahesh is a well-known evangelist and has preached to hundreds of thousands in Africa and seen twenty-five thousand come to the Lord at one time.

Mahesh told us about a time he was preaching in Africa when he felt the clear wind of the Holy Spirit come on him. God told him there was a man at the meeting whose son had died that morning, yet God was going to raise him from the dead. Mahesh spoke this word to the crowd, and a man came running forward. Mahesh prayed for him, and the Lord resurrected his son in the hospital.[2] Then he explained why he was telling us this:

> When I came here this week, I came into an atmosphere of the Holy Spirit that...it was like, I had not seen anything yet. This anointing is even purer and more glorious than what I had experienced.

One night during the time Mahesh was here, he was touched by God all night long. From that time, he relates:

> He told me to tell the pastors to dream great dreams. He is so great. We have not had a revelation of His greatness. It's no longer time for just a few superstars, but Jesus is *the* Superstar.
>
> God just wants to commission an army who will go out from here — an army of thousands who will resurrect the dead. Not just a few, but a new realm of God's anointing that He is loosening on earth right now.

We are seeing virtually every nation and denomination coming to worship God together and seek Him for more of

His blessing. Not only are all different denominations coming, including the Anglicans, Catholics, Pentecostals and Baptists, but we have also noticed that there is very little competition among any of the churches locally.

In Toronto, we are in relationship with about four hundred different churches from southern Ontario who are a part of the Metro and Ontario Renewal Network. This group is planing cooperative ways in which to spread renewal across the city of Toronto and beyond.

Often a group of churches will form a steering committee and invite Carol and me to come visit. Such is the case with Ché Ahn in Pasadena, California, and the recent Catch the Fire conference in Dallas, Texas. Similarly, it was a group of diverse churches that invited Randy Clark to Melbourne, Florida, that began meetings there.

What's happening in the U.K. is a story in itself, with churches uniting for renewal and different denominations getting together for large nation-shaking events. Christians are uniting in similar ways in Australia and New Zealand.

Major changes in the renewal since its beginning are the widespread expansion and increasing intensity. At first there was a wave of criticism that slowed things down in the United States, but I think the critics have, for the most part, been answered. Guy Chevreau pointed out that the very same issues that are raised today by the critics were in fact wonderfully answered by Jonathan Edwards 250 years ago. New apologetics have been written as well, such as *A True Revival* by Don Williams Ph.D. and *Renewal Apologetics* by Derek Morphew Ph.D. from South Africa.

By May 1994 the secular press picked up on the story, particularly in the U.K., and for the most part have written and given very favorable media reports. This has informed more and more people what is going on. It has helped pique the interest of thousands around the globe. In addition, thousands of leaders are traveling and "spreading the fire," both in large conferences in many nations, as well as in literally thousands of local churches throughout these nations.

Articles and books supporting the renewal are abounding, such as Chevreau's *Catch the Fire* and dozens of others. In addition, fifty to sixty top leaders have been touched in a powerful way; even some who were initially against it are now in total support of it — and the fire is blazing out of control. All I can say to that is, "Have mercy on us, Lord, and give us more."

I think that proportionately we are seeing increasing conversions. There is an increase in physical healings as well. The anointing is increasing, and more and more centers of renewal are opening up. Glowing reports from both individuals as well as churches continue to pour in. As the critics are answered and the fear of deception is dialed down in God's people, I see an increasing hunger for personal renewal as well as a growing desire to serve in the kingdom in many and varied ministries. More, Lord!

> For the earth will be filled with the knowledge of the glory of the Lord, as the waters cover the sea (Hab. 2:14).

THE HARVEST IS COMING

God is indeed raising up an army, full of love and grace and the Holy Spirit. Suddenly a trumpet will sound: "Go forth and bring in the harvest," and the church will see a victory like we have not seen in two thousand years. It's coming. I believe a great and abundant harvest is at hand.

Consider the following four scriptures:

> The harvest is the end of the age, and the harvesters are angels (Matt. 13:39).

In this life, good and evil co-exist together. But at the time of the end, there will be a great harvest in which even angels are involved.

> Then another angel came out of the temple and called in a loud voice to him who was sitting on the cloud, "Take your sickle and reap, because the time to reap has come, for the harvest of the earth is ripe." So he who was seated on the cloud swung his sickle over the earth, and the earth was harvested (Rev. 14:15-16).

These scriptures clearly teach that a massive harvest will indeed come in supernaturally during the end times.

> He told them, "The harvest is plentiful, but the workers are few. Ask the Lord of the harvest, therefore, to send out workers into his harvest field" (Luke 10:2).

Jesus is saying that the harvest is abundant, but the laborers are few. The saints of God, the born-again church, are the ones called as harvesters, and we are to pray that God will raise us up.

Some do not hold in faith the expectation for this harvest. They are expecting things to get worse and worse. They have a "hold the fort" mentality in which the small remnant of the church is to hang on until rescued by the rapture.

A lady in Switzerland asked me about this very issue. "Doesn't the Bible teach that there will be a great falling away?" I assured her it did, but asked her, "Don't you think we are in that time right now?" The once "Christian" West is now almost totally secular-humanist in its beliefs. If that's not a great falling away, then I don't know what is. We've had the great falling away. We're in it.

But God has promised us a harvest. I believe that in the

last days there will be a glorious, overcoming church that will be on the job to bring in the harvest. He will find faith on the earth when He returns! The gates of hell will not prevail!

In the third world nations, the evangelical church is growing tremendously. Ralph Winter and the U.S. Center for World Mission report that one out of seven in the world today is an evangelical Christian. This ratio is higher than ever before in history and increasing rapidly.

Now, finally, in the Western nations also, the Spirit of God is again moving like He has not moved in ninety years since the Pentecostal revival swept the earth. In our meetings in Toronto, we have witnessed thousands of believers being transformed by the power of God, strengthened and healed and becoming ready for Christian service. The blessing is spreading rapidly into every nation and denomination.

God is up to something big. I believe it is the greatest harvest of souls the world has ever seen.

PASS IT ON

This new move of the Spirit is for everybody, not just pastors and leaders. This is the ministry of the body of Christ. The Holy Spirit wants to fill you and enable you to take this renewal everywhere you go — not being weird or super-spiritual, but being "naturally supernatural." In the course of going to work and going to school, you can share your faith out of the power of this anointing and the love of Christ.

A man visiting our meetings from England wrote that while he was resting in the Spirit on the floor, he heard a voice repeating, "Give it away." He confessed that he feared attempting to "give it away" in case it did not work.

Upon leaving the building that night, he was stopped by a woman who asked, "Aren't you going to give it away?"

That did it for him. He prayed for her and her husband, and to his astonishment, the man fell to the floor and had an experience with God. This man is convinced now to give it away.

We are called to be faithful stewards of the things of God, and He is offering them to us freely and in abundance. When people come to our meetings or to a similar one elsewhere, they can soak in the anointing. If they continue to receive the Holy Spirit's presence and power, He will fill them to overflowing and transform them. When they go home and begin to minister, the same anointing goes home with them.

The Holy Spirit is falling like fire on the church, and when you and I catch fire, it begins burning in our hearts. When we minister to others, they, too, can catch the same fire and anointing we have. It burns in their hearts, and it multiplies to others. Such is the nature of this Person called the Holy Spirit.

We are saying, "Oh, Holy Spirit, we are not satisfied with what we have. It is wonderful. You have increased the anointing. You have increased the power, but oh God, let there be more. Let people be so filled with You that we will see the lame walk, the blind see, the deaf hear, the dead raised and the poor of the world have the gospel preached to them." That is where the heart of the Father wants to take us.

Your full potential is to go out and do the work that Jesus did (John 14:12). Press in with us. Receive the Father's blessing, then go for the kingdom and spread the fire!✪

NOTES

Chapter 2
The Fellowship of the Holy Spirit

1. *The New Strong's Exhaustive Concordance of the Bible* (Nashville, Tenn.: Thomas Nelson, 1984), Greek Dictionary of the New Testament, #4151.

2. *The New Strong's Exhaustive Concordance of the Bible* (Nashville, Tenn.: Thomas Nelson, 1984), Greek Dictionary of the New Testament, #3875.

Chapter 4
Evaluating This Move of God

1. Guy Chevreau, *Catch the Fire* (Toronto: HarperCollins, 1994), p. 116.

2. Ibid., pp. 82-83.

3. Ibid., p. 83.

4. Ibid., pp. 109-110.

Chapter 5
Decently and in Order

1. See Gen. 15:1; 26:24; Ex. 20:20; Josh. 8:1; Judg. 6:23.

2. Craig Rairdin and Parson's Technology Inc., QUICKVerse (Hiawatha, Iowa: Parson's Technology, 1992-1994).

Chapter 7
Fears: Roadblocks to Receiving

1. Words from song "How Big Is God?" by Stuart Hamblen, copyright 1959. Sheet music available from Hamblen Music Co., Box 1937, Santa Clarita, California 91386.

2. Teaching tape "Confessions of a Pharisee" by Jack Taylor can be obtained through the Toronto Airport Vineyard bookstore, 272 Atwell Dr., Toronto, Ontario, Canada M9W 6M3.

Chapter 10
The Phenomena: Revelations of Who God Is

1. Albert Farges, *Mystical Phenomena* (London: Burns Oates and Washbourne, 1926), p. 155.

2. Eddie Ensley, *Sounds of Wonder* (Mahwah, N.J.: Paulist Press, 1977), p. 94

3. *The New Strong's Exhaustive Concordance of the Bible* (Nashville, Tenn.: Thomas Nelson, 1984), Greek Dictionary of the New Testament, #1411.

4. Heather and Monica have seen God heal many people of their learning disabilities. A few people have had angelic visions, many have seen God doing something with their brain, and some have not seen anything but did experience God's healing. Heather and Monica know they serve a really big God! If you would like more information, you may contact Pastor Graham Harvey at the Vineyard Christian Fellowship, P.O. Box 754, Hopkinsville, Kentucky 42241, phone: (502) 885-7414; fax: (502) 886-6640.

Chapter 15
Spreading the Fire

1. Statistics from the World Evangelization Research Center, P.O. Box 129, Rockville, Virginia 23146.

2. A full account of the testimony of the resurrection is available in Mahesh Chavda's autobiography, *Only Love Can Make a Miracle*, available through Mahesh Chavda Ministries, P.O. Box 472009, Charlotte, North Carolina 28247, phone: (800) 730-6264.

BIBLIOGRAPHY

Chevreau, Guy. *Catch the Fire*. Toronto: HarperCollins, 1994.

DeArteaga, William. *Quenching the Spirit*. Lake Mary, Fla.: Creation House, 1992.

Deere, Jack. *Surprised by the Power of the Spirit*. Grand Rapids, Mich.: Zondervan, 1993.

Dixon, Patrick. *Signs of Revival*. Eastbourne, England: Kingsway, 1994.

Jackson, Bill. *What in the World Is Happening to Us?* This booklet of nineteen pages can be obtained through the Toronto Airport Vineyard bookstore, 272 Atwell Dr., Toronto, Ontario, Canada M9W 6M3.

Morphew, Derek. *Renewal Apologetics*. This position paper can be obtained through the Toronto Airport Vineyard bookstore, 272 Atwell Dr., Toronto, Ontario, Canada M9W 6M3.

White, John. *When the Spirit Comes With Power*. Westmont, Ill.: Intervarsity Press, 1988.

Williams, Don. *Revival — The Real Thing*. This booklet of fifty-four pages can be obtained through the Toronto Airport Vineyard bookstore, 272 Atwell Dr., Toronto, Ontario, Canada M9W 6M3.

THE TORONTO AIRPORT VINEYARD

John and Carol Arnott are the senior pastors of the Vineyard Christian Fellowship-Toronto Airport, also commonly known as Toronto Airport Vineyard. At the time of publication the Toronto Airport Vineyard is holding eighteen meetings per week.

- Sunday morning: Worship service

- Monday evening: Alpha
  (a course on evangelism)

- Tuesday through Sunday: Renewal
  meetings each evening

- Monday through Friday: Pastors and
  leaders' information meeting each morning

- Monday, Tuesday, Thursday and Friday:
  Prayer and intercession each afternoon

- Wednesday: Ontario Renewal Network
  (prayer/sharing with two hundred
  local pastors)

The Toronto Airport Vineyard has planted three new satellite churches since renewal started. The church has tripled in size from 360 members in 1994 to one thousand in regular attendance in 1995. It has a weekly outreach to help feed and clothe the homeless. A ministry training school for people age eighteen through thirty from around the world was established in September 1995. People will be trained in renewal and then sent to the nations or back home to plant churches and "fan the flames."

If you would like to contact the author
or learn more about the church
you may write or call:

Toronto Airport Vineyard
272 Atwell Dr.
Toronto, Ontario
Canada M9W 6M3

phone: (416) 674-8463 (VINE)
fax: (416) 674-8465

The official Vineyard Christian Fellowship
stance on the phenomena associated with
this renewal is available through:

Association of Vineyard Churches
P.O. Box 17580
Anaheim, California 92817
U.S.A.

If you enjoyed *The Father's Blessing,* we would like
to recommend the following books:

A Dream Come True
by James Ryle

James Ryle's gripping stories and profound biblical
insights give evidence that God still speaks in dreams
and visions. He shows from the Bible how God spoke
in dreams and how Christians today are still hearing God
speak the same way. He also offers a practical biblical
guide to interpreting your dreams.

Passion for Jesus
by Mike Bickle

Mike Bickle shares from his own life what it means to be
consumed with the personality of God. He challenges the
reader to discover the passion and splendor of God's
personality — a discovery that will help bring personal
wholeness and spiritual maturity. Understanding God's
heart will awaken our fervent devotion for Him.

Welcoming a Visitation of the Holy Spirit
by Wesley Campbell

Wesley Campbell offers a biblical explanation to this
move of the Holy Spirit that is sweeping the world.
Campbell's book goes beyond the meetings in Toronto
and examines similar moves of the Holy Spirit around
the world. He also offers guidelines for welcoming a
move of the Holy Spirit in your own life.

Available at your local Christian bookstore or from:

Creation House
600 Rinehart Road
Lake Mary, FL 32746
1-800-283-8494